The Immigrant

Guide to the

American Educational System

Stéphanie Mbella, Ph.D.

The Immigrant

Guide to the

American Educational System

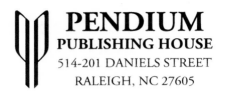

PENDIUM
PUBLISHING HOUSE
514-201 DANIELS STREET
RALEIGH, NC 27605

For information, please visit our Web site at
www.pendiumpublishing.com

PENDIUM Publishing and its logo
are registered trademarks.

The Immigrant Guide to the American Educational System
by Stéphanie Mbella

ISBN: 978-1-944348-37-3

PUBLISHER'S NOTE

This book is printed on acid-free paper.

CONTENTS

Dedication

To my mother, Victorine Ékè for all your love.

To my muse and sister, Clara Ékékè.

Acknowledgements

Special gratitude to Mrs. Cynthia Hammond-Davis.

Words of appreciation also go to all my supportive friends.

List of Tables

List of Figures

Note

The examples used throughout this book are actual instances of policies, requirements, and other elements of schools in the greater Washington DC Metropolitan Area (DMV), which is the home of a sizable community of African immigrants. However, the information provided could be applicable to much of the United States and relevant to anyone seeking to gain more knowledge about the American high school structure.

Introduction

The famous African and Malian writer Amadou Hampâté Ba once said, "When an old man dies, it is a library that burns." Depending upon whom you ask and the context in which these words are used, they can convey different meanings. By equating the death of an elderly symbol of wisdom to the destruction of a library symbol of knowledge, those words challenge Africans to sustain their *savoir-faire* and ensure that it gets transmitted to others in their community and to future generations.

Since the 1990s, the number of African immigrants settling in the United States has been growing steadily. Many migrate with their school-aged children, while others start their families in their host country. Regardless of their educational background prior to their arrival in the United States, African immigrants, with very few exceptions, struggle in understanding the educational system in which their offspring have to navigate. Reasons for this situation vary from one individual to another, from one country to another, and even from one region to another. After all, Africa is a continent, and her diversity translates into a myriad of educational systems. Few researchers have focused specifically on studying the African immigrant's experience within the American secondary school system. More often than not, based upon the educational data provided by students and parents, Africans are lumped into the same bandwagon as African-Americans and Caribbean natives, who, besides sharing a common ancestry, generally have different experiences with the American educational system.

As an educator, I have experienced firsthand the bewilderment and frustration of African students newly enrolled in the American secondary school system. I have seen parents lost, in need of answers, but afraid or embarrassed to ask questions because of the language barrier. Some prefer to stay away from fear of feeding into the stereotype of "stupid Africans" widely broadcasted by the Western media worldwide. I have seen parents angry at the power dynamics shift occurring with their children becoming more knowledgeable of the educational system and keeping them away from their academic lives. I have seen students wrongly advised by staff, thereby delaying their graduation in a timely manner. Some high school counselors are overwhelmed by the sheer size of their caseloads, which in some schools approximate 300 students per academic year. In this context, the most vulnerable students particularly those with language barriers, special needs, or without strong advocacy skills are more likely to receive insufficient and/or inaccurate information during the advising process. Moreover, some counseling professionals are prejudiced against minorities students. They hold low expectations for African Americans and Latinos and indirectly for Africans to achieve academic success in high school. These individuals confirm their erroneous assumptions by purposefully steering minorities students away from a college-bound track. Consequently, some students have to sign up for online after school courses to graduate on time. Such situations should be the exception rather than the norm among African immigrants. They should be an exception because there is ample information available on how to navigate the American secondary school system. In fact, there is even an overload of information in that regard disseminated across a variety of platforms. Surprisingly, in the 21st century, where, by a single mouse click or a quick keystroke on a laptop, tablet, smartphone, you can retrieve information for various purposes, few people are willing to use their research skills, mental stamina, and focus abilities to acquire the necessary information they need to make informed decisions.

That is where this guide steps in. Its purpose is not to provide an opinion on the American educational system. It stays away from upholding or castigating decisions made or ongoing debates to improve the educational system in the United States at the federal, state, or local levels. Rather, its content aims at empowering parents in their decision-making process as it relates to the academic endeavors of their offspring. To be even more specific, the information provided herein is primarily relevant to high school students.

As we move forward, I must emphasize a word of caution. This text is not a panacea to all the challenges faced by African immigrants, both parents and students alike, newly introduced to the American educational system. Although the list of topics remains general in nature, this compilation is neither exhaustive nor intended to be. Remember, the United States is a federal government; therefore, education is influenced to varying degrees by federal, state, and local governments. Therefore, it remains the responsibility of each parent to exercise some due diligence and take the necessary steps to inquire, study, and understand the intricacies of the school district where his or her son or daughter is enrolled in so that he or she gets the best the American education system has to offer.

Looking at the growing African community in the United States, specifically in the greater Washington DC Metropolitan area, Hampâté Ba's statement resonates with me. If we Africans want to have an influence in American sociey that is comparable other immigrant communities, we need to encourage the acquisition of a quality education for our younger brothers and sisters. Indeed, quality education grants access to better opportunities in life. It is up to all of us African professionals who at times walked on hot coals to integrate successfully into American society to lay out a solid and sustainable foundation so that our collective and rich libraries are not ruined.

Chapter 1

Overview of the American High School System

Most of the educational systems present in African countries reflect the educational traditions and requirements of their former colonizers. Thus, vestiges of German, French, British, Belgian, Spanish, Portuguese, and Italian educational systems are found across the continent. Officially, the United States held no colonies in Africa. Therefore, unless a parent has a child who previously attended an American school in their home country, there is some period of adjustment to understand its structure and its operation. This chapter provides a snapshot of the American school system with an emphasis on high school or the last four years of secondary school.

A. Types of Schools

The American secondary education landscape is as diverse as the country itself. The most common institutions in charge of educating youth belong to one of the following categories: public schools, private schools, home schools, and online schools.

Public Schools

Primarily financed by taxpayers' dollars, these schools fall under the authority of a school district.

• Regular public schools

The vast majority of the schools in the United States are public schools. The bulk of the children from immigrant families attend these institutions. In the Washington DC metropolitan area, they service students within their neighborhoods. Attendance at public schools depends on the county and the zip code of residence. In other words, a student can only enroll in his or her assigned school. For illustration purposes, let's first take the case of Montgomery County in the state of Maryland. A student and his or her parents must reside in that geographical area in order for the child to attend a school within that district. Therefore, students living in neighboring Prince George's County or Howard County are not eligible to attend Montgomery County Public Schools. Second a student is enrolled at a school based on the neighborhood in which he or she lives. If we stay within Montgomery County in Maryland, a student residing in Germantown is not eligible to attend a school located for example in Silver Spring. Schools with specific programs where students from the entire county congregate for their education are exempt from these restrictive rules. In that vein, students from Montgomery County enrolled in a technical or career pathway in high school could, at one time in their academic endeavor, attend Edison Technical High School in Silver Spring to complete their education.

Similarly, in the neighboring state of Virginia, student enrollment in schools depends on geographical boundaries. Thus, students residing in Fairfax County are not eligible to enroll in neighboring Arlington County. Within Fairfax County, middle or lower-level schools are clustered around a high school pyramid. Specifically, each high school gets its students from schools within its specific vicinity. For instance, students enrolled at Mount Vernon High School not only reside in Region 3 within the school boundaries map, but they most likely come from Whitman Middle School, which is a feeder school for Mount Vernon High School. Likewise, students from Falls Church High School in Region 2 reside in the city carrying the same name and transfer from Jackson Middle School.

This explanatory section wraps up with Washington DC. The federal capital of the United States is divided into four quadrants: northeast, northwest, southeast, and southwest. At the legislative level, the city boasts eight divisions, called wards. Akin to policies in place in neighboring Maryland and Virginia, students must attend schools within their assigned boundaries. Pupils who reside in Ward I should stay within that ward to complete their secondary school education. This compartmentalization of secondary schools is a core characteristic of the local American educational system African parents should grasp clearly.

- Public charter schools

These schools are public schools run independently from the larger public school district. Equally held to high standards for students' achievement, they are granted some leverage over their students' educational experience. Simply put, charters schools can indulge in new and alternative approaches of teaching as long as they meet the standards set by the school district. Washington DC houses many charters schools, some of which are private. According to the DC Public Charter School Board, the District is home to 118 public schools operated by 65 nonprofits and servicing 39,000 students from pre-k to 12th grade. Some charter schools require a complete application for admission. It is not uncommon for admission to a charter school to be secured via a lottery system.

Private Schools

In addition to the government, private entities are involved in the provision of a quality education in the United States. Within this category, the most widely known are religious schools, international schools, and college preparatory schools.

Often times, the admission process into a private high school mirrors that of a college. Prospective students are expected to complete an online application and submit supplemental materials including an essay, recommendation letters from previous English and math teachers, a transcript, standardized test scores, and in some cases, an interview and a site visit might be required prior to the final selection. The cost of private institutions can be a deterrent for some parents. Even though some of these institutions offer some forms of financial aid and renewable scholarships to students, parents should schedule an appointment with a financial advisor at the school of interest to examine the payment options before moving forward with the application process. In fact, most of the private schools offer payment plans for parents who choose this educational option for their offspring. The cost of attendance including tuition, fees, lunch, books, uniforms, and transportation can be even higher for international applicants.

Schools	City	State	Gender	Application	Entrance Exams	Interview	Tuition
National Cathedral School	Washington	DC	Female	Online	SSAT or ISEE	Yes	$40, 575
Bullis School	Potomac	MD	Co-ed	Online	SSAT or ISEE	Yes	$39,669
Potomac School	McLean	VA	Co-ed	Online	SSAT or ISEE	Yes	$38,550

Table 1: Sample tuitions for private schools in the DC Area 2016-2017

Some private schools also serve as boarding schools. Financial aid is available for eligible families. However, they must submit their application and all required materials by the deadline.

Schools	City	State	Gender	Application	Entrance Exams	Interview	Tuition
St Albans School	Washington	DC	Male	Online	SSAT[1] or ISEE[2]	Yes	$59,892
Georgetown Preparatory School	North Bethesda	MD	Male	Online	SSAT	Yes	$58,445
The Madeira School	McLean	VA	Female	Online	SSAT or ISEE	Yes	$58,158
Episcopal High School	Alexandria	VA	Co-ed	Online	SSAT	Yes	$54,250

Table 2: Sample tuitions for private boarding schools in the DC Area 2016-2017

- Religious schools

By far, the majority of religiously affiliated high schools in the United States are Catholic. They can be found across the Washington DC metropolitan area where they cater to the educational needs of a diverse student body. At times tuition might be lower for Catholic families although these institutions embrace students from all religious backgrounds. For instance, at Paul VI High School in Fairfax, VA the tuition for a Catholic student is $13,925 and $18,615 for a non-Catholic student. Still in Virginia, tuition for a Catholic student at Saint John Paul the Great High School is $12,780 and $16,480 for a non-Catholic student. It is important to mention that the cost of tuition per child decreases should a second or third child from the same family matriculate to either of those two high schools. Families who qualify for financial aid are encouraged to apply early to help pay for the cost of attendance. In the same vein, students can offset the high cost of their education by earning scholarships. Parents should contact the school of interest for their application and enrollment processes. Entrance exams might be scheduled on specific dates. Both application fees and deadlines vary from school to school. Upon acceptance, parents should be prepared to make a reservation fee to confirm their child's commitment to attend the school for the academic year he or she was admitted for. The enrollment deposit can be applied towards the student's tuition depending upon the policies of the school.

Schools	City	State	Gender	Application	Entrance Exams	Tuition
Stone Ridge School of Sacred Heart	Bethesda	MD	Female	Online	SSAT	$32,300
St Anselm's Abbey School	Washington	DC	Male	Online	OLSAT[3] and SCAT[4]	$26,900
Bishop McNamara High School	Forestville	MD	Co-ed	Online	HSPT[5]	$14,540
Paul VI High School	Fairfax	VA	Co-ed	Online/Print	HSPT	$13,925
Archbishop Carroll High School	Washington	DC	Co-ed	Online/Print	HSPT	$13,146
Saint John Paul The Great High School	Dumfries	VA	Co-ed	Online	HSPT	$12,780

Table 3: Sample tuitions for Catholic high schools in the DC Area 2016-2017

By Stéphanie Mbella

- International schools

Some schools offer a foreign education on American soil. These outward-oriented institutions are much more common in larger metropolitan areas with a high concentration of international institutions, diplomatic representations, and corporations with global outreach. Washington DC, New York City, Chicago, and Los-Angeles fall under this league where British, German, and French high schools cater to the needs of international students.

The British International School of Washington DC recommends a visit with a member of the admissions team and a site tour prior to the beginning of the enrollment process. Furthermore, this meeting provides parents with an opportunity to acquaint themselves with the academic terms, the curriculum, and the uniform policies. Tuition is based on the grade level of the student. For the 2016-2017 school year, the cost of attendance for high school students ranges from $30,585 to $32,255. This amount doesn't include fees. Payment is done online or via wire transfer. An enrollment deposit of $2,000 is required and applied towards the tuition.

Akin to the British School, prospective parents of the German School are advised to schedule an appointment for a campus tour. It can be done online or via phone. Admissions are done on a rolling basis and applications are accepted via mail, email, or they can be dropped off at the school. High school tuition ranges from $19,570 for 9th graders to $20,135 for 10th, 11th, and 12th graders. The school offers monthly and semi-annual payments options plan. Parents would have to sign-up for that service. Furthermore, financial aid is available to eligible families.

Lycée Rochambeau is the French International School in the Washington DC area. All students coming from a school not accredited by the French Ministry of Education must take an entrance exam in French and math. Families of prospective students must contact the admissions department to set up an appointment to start with the enrollment process. The school collects a $1,750 non-refundable and non-deductible first time enrollment fee per family. The tuition for high school students is $21,905. It is collected through the FACTS tuition

Management Company. Financial aid is available and allocated to eligible families who apply as per the school's guidelines.

Schools	City	State	Highest Tuition	Financial aid	Enrollment Fee
British International School of DC	Washington	DC	$32,255	No	$2,000
German School	Potomac	MD	$20,135	Yes	$2,000
Lycée Rochambeau	Bethesda	MD	$21,905	Yes	$1,000

Table 4: Sample tuitions for international high schools in the DC Area 2016-2017

College Preparatory Schools/College Prep Schools

College preparatory schools, which focus on college readiness can be public, private, or religiously affiliated. Some are co-educational, while others are single-gendered. Without exception, all these schools claim to prepare students for success in college and beyond. Given the variety in this field, it is up to each parent to research the school and especially the content of the curriculum to ensure that his or her child gets what has been advertised. In general, college preparatory schools focus on the academic readiness of students. Students are enrolled in Honors, Advanced Placement (AP) and International Baccalaureate (IB) Courses that would equip them with the academic, critical thinking and analytical skills expected from college students. Moreover, these institutions enable students to enroll in college level courses. Students participating in such dual enrollment programs i.e. taking simultaneously high school and college courses start to earn college credits towards a Bachelor's Degree. Another feature of college prep schools is to prepare students for the college entrance standardized tests, ACT and/or SAT, and ensure that pupils earn college ready scores. Some college prep schools have advisory groups through which students learn to navigate the college application and the financial aid processes. The goal of the advisory group is to empower students in their decision-making method as in college they would have to take ownership of their education and assess the pros and cons of each personal choice concerning their future.

By Stéphanie Mbella

Home Schools

Not all American students are educated in school buildings. Some are educated at home by parents or guardians. Though this may come as a surprise to some immigrants, home schooling is quite common in American culture. For the 2011-2012 school year, the US Department of Education's National Center for Education Statistics (NCES) found that 3% of the school aged population (5 to 17 years old) or more than 1 million students were homeschooled. A demographic breakdown of this student population indicates that 83% were white, 7% Hispanic, 5% Black, and 2% Asian or Pacific Islander. Statistics released by the Maryland State Department of Education for the 2009-2010 academic year and reported by Hand in Hand Education estimated at 2,734 the numbers of homeschooled students in Montgomery County and 2,991 in Prince George's County. Over the years, these figures have been declining as more students rejoin local public schools. In Washington DC, a Washington Post article noted the rise of homeschooling families from 209 in the 2013-2014 school year to 400 in the fall of 2015. The organization of Virginia Homeschoolers maintains annual statistics on homeschoolers per grade within the school districts. For 2014-2015, 48 high schoolers in Arlington County Public Schools were home schooled, 638 in Fairfax County Public Schools, and 365 in Prince William County Public Schools. Parents interested in this form of education for their children should give official notification to the State and the school district in which they reside. Such communication ensures that they meet the State and school district requirements. Furthermore, they should connect with organizations promoting homeschool as they might provide additional resources to better educate their child.

Online Schools

The education sector has not been spared by the technological leaps of the past decades. Currently, there are online programs that provide education to school-aged students all the way to high school. Such schools must be accredited by specific accrediting agencies rather than a school district.

Across the US, there are six regional accreditation agencies for elementary and secondary schools.

Schools accreditation agencies	States/Areas served
Middle States Association of Schools and Colleges, the Commission on Elementary and Secondary Schools (CESS-MSA)	Delaware, Maryland, New Jersey New York, Pennsylvania, Washington DC, US Virgin Islands
New England Association of Schools and Colleges (NEASC) Commission on Independent Schools (CIS)	Connecticut, Maine, Massachusetts, New Hampshire, Rhode Island
North Central Association Commission on Accreditation and School Improvement (NCA-CASI)	Arkansas, Arizona, Colorado, Illinois, Indiana, Iowa, Kansas, Michigan, Minnesota, Missouri, Nebraska, New Mexico, North Dakota, Ohio, Oklahoma, South Dakota, West Virginia, Wisconsin, Wyoming
Northwest Accreditation Commission (NWAC)	Alaska, Idaho, Montana, Nevada, Oregon, Utah, Washington
Southern Association of Colleges and Schools Council on Accreditation and Schools Improvement (SACS CASI)	Alabama, Florida, Georgia, Kentucky, Louisiana, Mississippi, North Carolina, Tennessee, Texas
Western Association of Schools and Colleges (WASC) Accrediting Commission for Schools (ACS)	California, Hawaii, Guam, America Samoa, Pacific Islands

Table 5: Regional accreditation agencies

The State of Maryland and Washington DC fall under the purview of the Middle States Association of Schools and Colleges, the Commission on Elementary and Secondary Schools (MSA-CESS). The Virginia Council on Private Education (VCPE) monitors the accreditation status of all private elementary and secondary schools in the State. Parents interested in online education for their high school child should contact the appropriate agency for guidance and to ensure that this option would be the most rewarding for the family unit.

B. Grade Levels

The difference in terminology often accentuates the confusion of African parents in understanding the grade level equivalency with the American high school system. To avoid the confusion, parents must keep in mind that in most countries of the world, secondary school education in its entirety averages seven years long. In the United States, the first three years are called middle school, and the last four years high school. Each grade level in high school carries a specific name: freshman, sophomore, junior, and senior. French and British educational systems have evolved in their former African colonies. However, the following comparative table is based on the most common and simplistic descriptions of those respective secondary school systems. It might be slightly different from one African country to the other, but ultimately it serves to enlighten parents' understanding of the grade level equivalent in the American system.

Educational Systems	American System		French System	British System[6]
Grade Levels				
Middle School		Sixth Grade (6th Grade)	Sixième (6e)	First Year
		Seventh Grade (7th Grade)	Cinquième (5e)	Second Year
		Eight Grade (8th Grade)	Collège Quatrième (4e)	Third Year
High School	Freshman	Ninth Grade (9th Grade)	Troisième (3e)	Fourth Year
	Sophomore	Tenth Grade (10th Grade)	Seconde (2nde)	Fifth Year
	Junior	Eleventh Grade (11th Grade)	Lycée Première (1ère)	Sixth Year
	Senior	Twelfth Grade (12th Grade)	Terminale (Tle)	Seventh Year

Table 6: Grade levels equivalency between American, French, and British secondary school systems

C. Courses: Core and Electives

During their studies, high school students must take two types of courses: core courses and electives courses. Within a specific curriculum, core courses refer to those general education classes required of all students for graduation purposes. Regardless of their areas of specialization, all students must take those courses. English, mathematics, social studies, and science fall in that group. Elective classes represent a list of courses offered in schools from which students can choose to meet their graduation requirements. These classes allow learners to explore some of their interests. Art, music, computer, journalism, business, and health are examples of elective subjects. To ensure that they graduate in a timely manner, students are encouraged to complete their core courses prior to their electives. Passing a core course determines the promotion to the next grade level. Therefore, parents should ensure that during the registration process, their children sign up for the proper classes. For further clarification about the enrollment procedure, parents should consult their children's school counselor to determine the proper course of action. During the meeting, parents might ask some of the suggested questions:

1. Is my child on track for graduation? Would my child need to make-up for classes to graduate on time?
2. What elective courses do you recommend for my child?
3. What Honors and/or AP courses do you recommend for my child?
4. Would my child enrollment in multiple Honors and/or AP Courses this year negatively affect his or her grades?
5. What is the withdrawal policy from a class should my child become overwhelmed by an AP course?
6. Given my child's academic background is there room for dual enrollment courses in his or her schedule as a junior or a senior?
7. What is the likelihood of my child having an abbreviated schedule as a senior?
8. Looking at my child's completed and future coursework how does he or she stand out among prospective college applicants?
9. What would my child need to improve his or her profile for college applications?
10. What else should we be doing now to prepare for the college application process?

These sample questions might act as icebreakers with counselors and help parents assess the alignment of their child coursework with his or her college preparation goals.

D. Academic Calendar

In general, American schools operate on a 10-month calendar. Classes begin from the middle to the end of the summer, depending upon the location and whether the school is on a designated year-round track. The school year concludes around the month of May or June of the following year. Many school systems in Africa operate in a similar manner with the school year beginning in September or early October and wrapping up in June or July. However, South Africa has an academic year that spans across the calendar from January to December. Parents should be aware that graduating seniors in high school wrap up their academic year some days earlier than their peers. In the DMV area public schools, the academic year is divided into four parts called marking periods in Montgomery County (Maryland); quarters in Prince George's County (Maryland); grading periods in Fairfax County (Virginia); and advisories in Washington DC. In the middle of each quarter, parents receive progress reports about their children's school performance. At the end of the semester, parents receive report cards via their students or regular mail.

Year-round schools equally belong to the educational landscape in the United States. The format varies depending upon the school's vision, resources, and enrollment size. The most common form is the 45-15 plan under which students attend school for 45 days and have a 15-day break. According to the National Education Association, other designs include the 60-20 and the 90-30 plans. Although most students attend schools with regular academic calendars, a growing percentage of parents enroll their offspring in year-round schools. Some parents perceive this option as a solution to summer idleness. Others view it as a means for maximizing the use of the school infrastructure.

E. School Day

In spite of differences in the official starting time, the high school day averages 6.5 to 7.0 hours. In Washington DC, students report to school from 8:45am to 3:15pm. In neighboring Maryland, the school day goes from 7:45am to 2:30pm in Montgomery County. In Prince George's County, the bell schedule is scattered as high schools start times range between 7:45am and 9:30am and end between 2:25pm to 4:10pm. Likewise, in Virginia's Fairfax County Public Schools, most high schools run from either 8:00am to 2:45pm or 8:10am to 2:55pm. Exceptions would not be an anomaly as schools might function under particular circumstances. It is worth emphasizing that inclement weather or special conditions can change that structure. In that regard, parents should become familiar with the terms "two-hour delay" and "early release."

In the Washington DC metropolitan area, two-hour delays commonly occur due to snow, ice, or other weather-related events. Exceptionally, students report to school two hours after their official starting time. Parents and students should sign-up with the school alert system to be kept abreast of such changes. During early release, classes start as scheduled but the school day is shortened. Students are dismissed after lunch. Early release dates are captured on the school calendar provided to parents at the beginning of the school year. For both instances, parents need to secure transportation for students not commuting with school buses.

F. Periods: Length of Classes

Though general guidelines exist, every school determines the duration of classes. In local high schools, classes vary between 45 minutes, 50 minutes, or 90 minutes long. Depending upon the length of classes, a student can have four, five, seven, or more periods (classes) in a day. At this point, two scenarios emerge. Students can have "an all period day" or a "regular block" day. Again, the terminology might differ from one school district to the other. In the first case scenario, a student has multiple but shortened classes throughout the day. In the second scenario, the time allocated to instruction in a period is longer with fewer classes to attend during the school day. Some schools use both systems alternatively. In other words, students might have some days of the week with shortened class sessions and others with lengthier class sessions. This information equally appears in the school's academic calendar provided to students and parents at the beginning of the school year. Grasping this information further provides parents with the tools to be involved in the academic lives of their children.

G. Books

Unlike in African countries where parents must purchase all books for their offspring, most students in American public schools are assigned books in their courses. Students and parents acknowledge receipt of the book by signing a form provided according to the school's protocol. It is the student's responsibility to take care of the book and ensure that it is returned in good condition at the end of the course. If the student returns the book in poor condition, he or she must replace it. Textbooks are very expensive, some costing more than one hundred dollars. It is in the best interest of students to be good stewards of the manuals entrusted to them.

H. Dress Code

Across Africa, most high school students wear a school uniform. For some, the impetus is to maintain equality among students irrespective of their family's economic status. While some in the United States embrace that philosophy, others prefer students wear their own clothing to reflect their personality. Nevertheless, across all schools, administrators enforce dress codes strictly so that students abide by specific parameters of decency. In cases where students wear a uniform, parents might have to purchase matching jackets for the colder months of the year.

I. Cafeteria

As public entities, public schools cater to the needs of all students regardless of financial background. In that logic, they get the opportunity to eat breakfast and lunch on campus. Menus are available for the parents to review and ensure compliance with their child's dietary restrictions. For equity purposes, students from lower income families can access the meals offered by their school cafeteria for a modest cost. However, at the beginning of the academic year, eligible parents must apply for the Free and Reduced Meal plans. Depending upon the circumstances, the qualified student either contributes a small fee for the meal of does not pay at all.

Lunch schedules and procedures vary from schools to school even within the same school district. Lunch times can be common, meaning that all students from 9th to 12th grades eat lunch at the same time without exception. Conversely, it can be scattered along grade levels. For example, a school might have three lunches. The first lunch is for their 9th graders, the second for their 10th graders, and the last for the 11th and 12th graders. Some schools might offer an "open lunch" during which students can leave the campus grounds to purchase food in the neighborhood. It is important for students to follow the school's guidelines for open lunches for safety and accountability purposes. Students are under the supervision of the school until the end of the school day. For students not eligible for Free and Reduced Meals, parents should keep up-to-date with funds in their student's cafeteria account or provide them daily with lunch money.

J. Transportation

Around the DMV area, most public school districts offer transportation to students to and from school. Students meet at specific pick-up locations where school buses carry them to their respective schools. Parents and students get the routes information and pick-up times during the enrollment process. Under some circumstances, schools use buses for after-school activities. Specifically, there are "late buses" provided to students to facilitate their return home after their attendance at extra-curricular activities on campus. Not all schools provide this accommodation. For some schools, this service is provided only on certain days of the week. In cases when their child is involved in activities that run beyond the late bus, it is up to parents or guardians to ensure proper transportation home to students. Exceptionally, in lieu of school buses, students might have youth passes or tokens they can use during school days to commute to and from school. Their use can be restricted to specific times. It is recommended that parents check with school staff on how to purchase these discounted fares for their offspring, and be informed about the times and identification constraints they could be associated with.

K. Attendance and Truancy

School attendance is compulsory for children between the ages of 5 to 16 years old. Parents should make sure that their children report to school on a regular basis. If for some reason a child has to miss school, it is their responsibility to notify the school. School administrators might consider students with excessive unexcused absences as determined by state law as truants. Truancy is a status offense. The school system's legal representative could summon parent and student to court to address this issue. The aim of this process is to ensure that the student resumes and successfully completes his or her education. At the beginning of the academic year, high school students usually receive agendas or planners highlighting their schools' policies, including those on attendance and truancy.

L. Discipline

Culturally, teachers in the African context have more leverage in addressing instances of students' misbehavior at their own discretion than teachers in American school systems do. African parents must come to terms that American teachers exercise very little power as far as discipline is concerned. Within American schools, specific individuals address discipline issues in accordance with the rules and regulations of the school system. Deans of discipline, security staff, counselors, and, at times, social workers are responsible for handling discipline issues; teachers have nothing to do with this aspect of student life. It thus becomes imperative for both parents and students to familiarize themselves with the guidelines that apply when students commit infractions and the length of time associated with each infraction. In any event, school staff must notify parents about each of the following major disciplinary issues:

- *Detention*: the student is to report at a specific day and time to an area in his or her school.
- *In-School Suspension or ISS*: for a short time, the student is prohibited from attending regular classes. He or she is to report on time to a designated location at the school, where he or she spends instructional time under the supervision of a staff member. There, the students complete their regular schoolwork, and the supervising staff member submits it to their teachers. The students' ability to receive credit for work done during ISS depends on the school system's policy.
- *Out of School Suspension or OSS*: the student is forbidden altogether to set foot on campus grounds. For the duration of his or her suspension, the student's parent or guardian must stop by the school and collect the student's work from either teachers or counselors, depending on the school's policy. The same policy dictates whether the student can get credit for this work. Sometimes, during this process, students with disabilities might be assigned to a specific school exclusively for students in such situations. Thus, they are not denied instruction under the Free and Appropriate Public Education (FAPE) law. The administrative team must ensure that the misbehavior exhibited by a special needs student was not caused by his or her disability.
- *Expulsion*: the student is banned from returning to his or her school. Students in this situation must deal with complex rules, and the legal system might become involved.

Takeaways from Chapter 1

This chapter provided a quick overview of the American education system particularly as it relates to high school students. In spite of similarities with various African educational systems, strong differences exist in terms of organization, terminology, and procedures used not only between school districts but also from one school to the next within a specific district. In this section, we covered the following points:

- A sizable number of secondary school aged African immigrants residing in the DMV area attend public schools.
- Enrollment at a school depends on the place of residency.
- American vocabulary aside, grade levels are equivalent to most school systems in Africa.
- School buses address the bulk of the transportation needs of students.
- Blocks and the number of classes students take per day are a function of their schools' vision.
- All books assigned to students in their classes must be returned at the end of each course or be replaced.
- In schools with a uniform policy, parents should purchase matching school jackets for colder months.
- Students from eligible families can qualify for free and reduced breakfast and lunch if they follow the prescribed guidelines at the beginning of the school year.
- School attendance is obligatory. Truancy is not an option.
- Discipline matters fall under the responsibility of specific staff at the school. Consequences for infractions are based on precise guidelines available to the public. However, parents must be notified for each disciplinary action their children incur.

Parent Only Worksheet – Chapter 1

Please select all that apply for your child

Key points	Available options
Types of school	☐ Public ☐ Private ☐ College Prep School ☐ Home school ☐ Online
Student grade level	☐ 9th ☐ 10th ☐ 11th ☐ 12th
Core courses this year	
Elective courses this year	
Block and classes	☐ Period 1 _____ ☐ Period 2 _____ ☐ Period 3 _____ ☐ Period 4 _____ ☐ Period 5 _____ ☐ Period 6 _____ ☐ Period 7 _____ ☐ Period 8 _____ ☐ Period 9 _____ ☐ Period 10 _____
Number of books assigned	☐ 1 ☐ 2 ☐ 3 ☐ 4 ☐ 5 ☐ 6 ☐ +7
Dress code	☐ Uniform ☐ No Uniform
Cafeteria options	☐ Free and Reduced Price Meals ☐ Regular Priced Meals
Transportation options	☐ Walk ☐ School Bus ☐ Public Transportation ☐ Car
Contact (s) for excused absence at school	

BY STÉPHANIE MBELLA

Name: _____ Grade: _____

Student Only Worksheet – Chapter 1

Questions	Answers
List all your core courses for this school year	_____ _____ _____ _____ _____ _____ _____ _____ _____ _____
List all your elective courses for this year	_____ _____ _____ _____ _____ _____ _____ _____
Number of periods per day	_____
When is your lunchtime?	Monday: _____ Tuesday: _____ Wednesday: _____ Thursday: _____ Friday: _____
Days for activity bus	☐ Monday ☐ Tuesday ☐ Wednesday ☐ Thursday ☐ Friday
Activity bus departure time	Monday: _____ Tuesday: _____ Wednesday: _____ Thursday: _____ Friday: _____

Record your school resources in the table below

Title	Name	Office Location	Office Phone
Principal			
School Counselor			
Grade Level Administrator			
Dean of Discipline/Head of Discipline			
Attendance Officer			
College and Career Center Coordinator			
SAT/ACT Testing Coordinator *(if applicable)*			
AP Testing Coordinator *(if applicable)*			
Dual Enrollment Coordinator			
ELL/ESOL Coordinator			
Nurse			
Coach *(if applicable)*			
Mentor *(if applicable)*)			
Case Manager *(if applicable)*			

Chapter 2

The Academic Picture

As in other parts of the world, earning a diploma marks the end of secondary school education in the United States. For Africans having studied in their countries, this completion translates into obtaining the General Certificate of Education (GCE) for some English-speaking countries or the *Baccalauréat* (Bac) in Francophone countries. In the US, there are minor differences they must grasp to make informed decisions.

A. Degrees

Three types of degrees are available to American high school students:

1) An International Baccalaureate Diploma, which provides secondary school credentials accepted by many institutions of higher education worldwide. The IB Program expands from the elementary years to the end of secondary school. Schools must undergo a stringent authorization process to become an IB school. In addition, they must pay annual costs to offer that curriculum to students.

School Districts	State	International Baccalaureate (IB) High Schools
Montgomery County Public Schools	Maryland	Bethesda-Chevy Chase; Albert Einstein; John F. Kennedy Richard Montgomery; Rockville; Seneca Valley; Watkins Mill
Prince George's County Public Schools	Maryland	Central; Crossland; Frederick Douglass; Laurel; Parkdale; Suitland
District of Columbia Public Schools	DC	Benjamin Banneker; Eastern Senior; British International School of Washington* (private international school)
Fairfax County Public Schools	Virginia	Annandale; Edison; Lee; Marshall; Mount Vernon; Robinson Stuart

Table 7: International Baccalaureate (IB) high schools in the DC Area
(SY 2016-2017)

2) A High School Diploma, which marks the end of high school and enables the transition into postsecondary institutions. The requirements include the successful completion of a curriculum, specific community service hours, and state standardized tests. Students with special needs can be on a diploma track depending upon their disability and their Individual Education Plans (IEPs).

3) High School Certificate
Legally, students with special needs are entitled to secondary school education until the age of 21. Students with severe disabilities could receive certificates of completion or certificates of attendance. In Virginia, a Certificate of Program Completion is awarded to students with disabilities who are not eligible for a diploma. Likewise, in Washington DC Public Schools, students with special needs who are not on a high school diploma track earn a Certificate of IEP Completion. The Maryland High School Certificate enables its holders to apply for enrollment at a Maryland Community College upon graduation from High School. Decisions about a certificate track or a diploma track for students with special needs are taken by the IEP team, which includes the parent/guardian of the student.

B. High School Pathways

Overall, when compared to American school systems, school pathways in African educational systems are more easily recognizable. Technical schools, career schools, and various pathways are optimally identified to reduce confusion during the school selection process. Thus, in Francophone countries, "Lycée Technique" refers to a high school where some of the career pathways offered to students might include a wide range of technical or vocational choices such as carpentry, automotive, plumbing, mechanics, Heat, ventilation, and air conditioning (HVAC), management, business, marketing, culinary arts, home economics, or even sowing. In Cameroon for example, it is not uncommon for students to begin their specialization upon their admission into secondary school, as early as the sixth grade. Although not as transparent in the United States educational system, this variety is equally present, however there is a twist. Unlike their African counterparts operating at times under specific mandates from national governments, American high schools can carve out, on their own volition, the distinctive study pathways they offer to students.

In general, high schools offer a broad curriculum to all students. In addition to that, they offer programs that distinguish one high school from the next and create some sort of niche or area of expertise upon which the school builds its reputation. Those programs within the school are managed under entities called academies, small learning communities (SLCs), signature programs, or areas studies. Rather than frowning upon these terms, immigrant parents should embrace them as diverse fields of studies available to their children. It is worth noting that entrance into some of these programs may require a particular application process. Middle schools students and parents should directly contact the high school of interest for the admissions requirements into these particular programs. High school open houses remain the best venue for parents and child to visit the campus, question current students and teachers about the program of interest, and examine the variety of academic support, student life, and community resources available to students.

For information purposes, the following tables highlight some of the special programs within some High Schools in the District, Maryland, and Virginia (DMV) area.

Schools	Ward	Special Programs
Ballou High School	8	Academy of Hospitality and Tourism
Cardozo Education Campus	1	Academy of Information Technology, JROTC, The International Academy, TransSTEM Academy
Duke Ellington School of the Arts	1	Arts, Dance, Instrumental Music, Literary Media & Communications, Museum Studies, Theater, Visual Arts, Vocal Music
Dunbar High School	5	STEM Academy, Academy for Careers in Education, Academy for Business and Public Policy
Eastern High School	6	Health and Medical Sciences Academy, JROTC

Table 8: Samples study pathways in some Washington DC Public Schools (School Year 2016-2017)

Schools	City	Special Programs
Montgomery Blair High School	Silver Spring	Entrepreneurship; Human Service Professions; International Studies and Law; Media, Music, and the Arts; Science, Technology, Engineering, and Math (STEM)
James Hubert Blake High School	Silver Spring	Fine Arts; Humanities; Science, Technology, Engineering, and Math (STEM)
Winston Churchill High School	Potomac	Mathematics, Technology, and Science; Creative and Performing Arts
Clarksburg High School	Clarksburg	Advanced Placement Power Scholars (APPS)
Damascus High School	Damascus	Academy of Information Technology (AOIT)
Thomas Edison High School of Technology	Silver Spring	Automotive; Construction; Human and Consumer Services
Albert Einstein High School	Kensington	Academy of Finance, Business, Management and Marketing; Academy of Visual and Performing Arts; Renaissance Academy
Gaithersburg High School	Gaithersburg	Arts and Communication; Business Studies; Leadership and Education; Science and Technology; Project Lead the Way: Biomedical Science Program
Walter Johnson High School	Bethesda	APEX Scholars
John F. Kennedy High School	Silver Spring	Broadcast Journalism and Communications; Business Management and Administration; Creative Multi-Media; Health Careers; Public Communications; Leadership Training Institute; Medical Careers; Naval Junior Reserve Officers' Training Corps (NJROTC)
Col. Zadok Magruder High School	Rockville	Academy of Finance; Project Lead the Way/Engineering; Early Childhood; Hospitality Management
Northwest High School	Germantown	Academy of Biotechnology; Academy of Fine Arts; Academy of Finance; Ulysses Signature Program

Schools	City	Special Programs
Northwood High School	Silver Spring	Academy of Musical Theatre and Dance; Academy of Politics, Advocacy and Law; Academy of Technological & Environmental Science Systems; Humanities, Arts & Media Academy
Paint Branch High School	Burtonsville	Academy of Media; Academy of Science; Academy of Finance; Academy of Engineering Technology; Academy of Health Professions; Academy of Restaurant Management & Culinary Arts; Academy of Child Development & Education; Naval Junior Reserve Officers' Training Corps (NJROTC)
Poolesville High School	Poolesville	Advanced Engineering Academy (Project Lead the Way)
Quince Orchard High School	Gaithersburg	Advanced Studies in Arts and Academics
Rockville High School	Rockville	Project Lead the Way (The Engineering Academy); Journalism
Seneca Valley High School	Germantown	Academy of Information Technology (AOIT); College Institute; Naval Junior Reserve Officers' Training Corps (NJROTC)
Sherwood High School	Sandy Spring	Academy of Health Professions; Television Production; Advanced Engineering (Project Lead the Way); Certified Professional Horticulturist; Early Child Development; Hospitality Management; Accounting (Business Program)
Springbrook High School	Silver Spring	Academy of Information Technology (AOIT); Justice, Law, and Society; Environmental Horticulture; Hospitality Management; Early Child Development
Watkins Mill High School	Gaithersburg	Academy of Engineering (Project Lead the Way); Academy of Finance; Academy of Hospitality; Medical Careers; Early Childhood Development
Wheaton High School	Silver Spring	The Biosciences Academy; Academy of Information Technology; Academy of Engineering; Institute for Global and Cultural Studies
Walt Whitman High School	Bethesda	Engineering (Project Lead the Way);
Thomas S. Wooton High School	Rockville	Humanities and Arts; Academy of Information Technology; Science, Technology, and Research Scholars (STARS); Education Academy

Table 9: Samples study pathways in Montgomery County Public Schools in Maryland (School Year 2016-2017)

Schools	City	Special Programs
Bladensburg High School	Bladensburg	Graphic Arts, Media, & Communication; Health & Biosciences; Hospitality & Tourism
Bowie High School	Bowie	Summit Scholar Program
Central High School	Capitol Heights	French Immersion Program; Law, Education & Public Service
Charles H. Flowers High School	Springdale	Academy of Finance; Science and Technology; Engineering (Project Lead the Way); Hospitality & Restaurant Management; Fire Science Cadet Program

Schools	City	Special Programs
Crossland High School	Temple Hills	Academy of Architecture and Design; Technical Academy (Accounting and Finance, Automotive Technician, Barbering, Business Management, Computer Networking, Cosmetology, Electrical, IT Essentials, Masonry, Heating, Ventilation, and Air Conditioning (HVAC))
Dr. Henry A. Wise High School	Upper Marlboro	Puma Pride Scholars Program; Air Force Junior Reserve Officer Training Corp (AFJROTC)
DuVal High School	Lanham	Aerospace Engineering & Aviation Technology; Consumer Service and Hospitality & Tourism; Graphic Arts, Media, Communication; Information Technology; Project Lead the Way
Eleanor Roosevelt High School	Greenbelt	Academy of Business & Finance; Science & Technology; AP Capstone
Fairmont Heights High School	Capitol Heights	Junior Reserve Officer Training Corps (JROTC),
Frederick Douglass High School	Upper Marlboro	Business; Family Consumer Sciences; Television Production
Friendly High School	Fort Washington	Advanced Placement Courses
Gwynn Park High School	Brandywine	Automotive Technology; Academy of Consumer Services, Hospitality & Tourism; Academy of Information & Technology; Academy of Environmental Studies
High Point High School	Beltsville	Homeland Security & Military Science; Environmental Science; Project Lead the Way (Engineering); Project Lead the Way (Computer Science); Child Development; Air Force Junior Reserve Officer Training Corps (AFJROTC)
Largo High School	Upper Marlboro	Academy of Finance; Academy of Health & Biosciences; Air Force Junior Reserve Officer Training Corps (AFJROTC)
Laurel High School	Laurel	Academy of Global Studies; Air Force Junior Reserve Officer Training Corps (AFJROTC)
Northwestern High School	Hyattsville	Academy of Business and Science; Academy of Engineering and Science; TV Production; NJROTC
Oxon Hill High School	Oxon Hill	Academy of Business and Finance; Academy of Engineering and Science; Academy of Graphic Arts and Media; Academy of Hospitality and Tourism; Academy of Military Science; Academy of Science and Technology;
Parkdale High School	Riverdale Park	Global Academy; Advance Placement Courses; JROTC
Potomac High School	Oxon Hill	Business; Homeland Security; Law & Public Service; Technology Education
Suitland High School	Forestville	Architecture and Design; Business and Finance; Consumer Services Hospitality and Tourism; Engineering and Science; Graphic Arts, Media, and Communication; Health and Biosciences; Homeland Security and Military Science; Transportation; Visual and Performing Arts
Surrattsville High School	Clinton	Academy of Law, Education, and Public Service; Academy of Law Graphic Art, Media and Communication

Table 10: Samples study pathways in Prince George's County Public Schools in Maryland (School Year 2016-2017)

BY STÉPHANIE MBELLA

The International School at Langley Park and the International School at Largo are new additions to the list of public high schools in Prince George's County. They cater primarily to immigrant students in the community.

Schools	City	Special Programs
Annandale High School	Annandale	Performing Arts; Fine Arts
Centreville High School	Clifton	Fine Arts; Performing Arts; Health and Medical Sciences; Technology & Engineering Education; Trade and Industrial
Chantilly High School	Chantilly	Governor's STEM Academy;
Edison High School	Alexandria	Animal Science; Automotive Collision Service; Automotive Technology; Cosmetology; Criminal Justice; Culinary Arts; Cyber: Computer Systems Technology; Electrical Construction & Engineering; Heating Ventilation & Air Conditioning (HVAC); Teachers for Tomorrow
Fairfax High School	Fairfax	Chinese; Dance; Fashion Careers; Korean; Music & Computer Technology; Professional Musical Theatre & Actor's Studio; Professional Photography Studio; Professional Television Production; Social Media Marketing
Falls Church High School	Falls Church	Health & Medical Courses (Biotechnology Foundations, Dental Careers, Fire & Emergency Medical Sciences, Medical Assistant, Pharmacy Technician); Human Services Courses (Criminal Justice, Early Childhood)
Herndon High School	Herndon	Advanced Placement Courses
Langley High School	McLean	Career & Technical Education; Performing Arts; Fine Arts
Lee High School	Springfield	Edison Academy: Animal Science; Automotive Collision Service; Automotive Technology; Cosmetology; Criminal Justice; Culinary Arts; Cyber: Computer Systems Technology; Electrical Construction & Engineering; Heating Ventilation & Air Conditioning (HVAC); Teachers for Tomorrow
Madison High School	Vienna	Advanced Placement Courses
Marshall High School	Falls Church	IT and Engineering; Cyber Security; STEM Robotics Systems; Automotive Technician; Chinese Language; Cosmetology; Criminal Justice; Culinary Arts; Entrepreneurship
McLean High School	McLean	Advanced Placement Courses
Oakton High School	Vienna	Art (Computer Graphics, Photography, Art Studio); Career and Technical Education (Business, Marketing, Technology/ Engineering)
South County High School	Lorton	Advanced Placement Courses
Thomas Jefferson High School	Alexandria	Research Labs (Astronomy & Physics; Automation & Robotics; Biotechnology & Life Science; Chemical Analysis & Nanochemistry; Communication Systems; Computer Systems; Energy Systems; Engineering Design; Mobile and Web Application Development; Neuroscience; Oceanography & Geographical Systems; Quantum Physics and Optics;
West Potomac High School	Alexandria	Advanced Placement Courses; JROTC

Schools	City	Special Programs
West Springfield High School	Springfield	Advanced Placement Courses
Westfield High School	Chantilly	Career & Technology Education (Business, Marketing, Technology and Engineering, Trade & Industrial)
Woodson High School	Fairfax	Advanced Placement Courses

Table 11: Samples study pathways in Fairfax County Public Schools in Virginia (School Year 2016-2017)

C. High School Magnet Programs

Some schools offer a unique curriculum focused on a theme or a special area of study. The variety of courses offered aligns with academic standards. Students attending these programs might come from a larger geographic area within the school district. With the application process following specific and, at times, very strict guidelines, parents and middle school students alike should contact the magnet program coordinator at the school the student wants to attend. Moreover, parents and students should attend open houses and other public informational sessions to ascertain their choices. The following tables list of some magnet programs in selected schools within the DMV area.

Program	Schools
Biomedical Magnet Program	Wheaton High School
Career Programs	Thomas Edison High School
Communication Arts Program (CAP)	Montgomery Blair High School
Engineering Magnet Program	Wheaton High School
Global Ecology	Poolesville High School
Humanities House	Poolesville High School
International Baccalaureate Diploma Programme	Richard Montgomery High School
Leadership Training Institute	John F. Kennedy High School
Science, Math, and Computer Science Magnet	Montgomery Blair High School
Science, Math, and Computer Science Magnet	Poolesville High School
Visual Art Center	Albert Einstein High School

Table 12: Sample high school magnet programs in Montgomery County in Maryland (School Year 2016-2017)

Program	Schools
Biomedical Program	Bladensburg High School
French Immersion Program	Central High School
Science and Technology	Eleanor Roosevelt High School
Biotechnology Program	Fairmont Heights High School
Science and Technology	Charles Herbert Flowers High School
Biotechnology Program	Largo High School
Science and Technology	Oxon Hill High School
Visual and Performing Art Magnet Program	Suitland High School

Table 13: Sample high school magnet programs in Prince George's County in Maryland (School Year 2016-2017)

Program	Schools
International Baccalaureate	Benjamin Banneker Academy High School
Advance Placement Courses	Columbia Heights Educational Campus
Art, Dance, Theatre, Visual Arts, Vocal Music	Duke Ellington School of the Arts
Biotechnology, Engineering, Information Technology	McKinley Technology High School
Architecture, Engineering, Welding, HVAC/R, Plumbing, Electrical	Phelps Architecture, Construction, and Engineering High School
Humanities, Advanced Placement Courses	School without Walls Senior High School

Table 14: Sample high school magnet programs in the District of Columbia (School Year 2016-2017)

Program	Schools
Science and Technology, Math and Computer Science, Research Program	Thomas Jefferson High School for Science and Technology

Table 15: Sample high school magnet programs in Fairfax County in Virginia (School Year 2016-2017)

D. Graduation Requirements

To graduate from high school, students must meet the minimum state, school district, and at times school requirements to graduate. These conditions are commonly in place when the student first enters 9th grade.

Maryland

Maryland law mandates that high school students earn a minimum of 21 credits to graduate. While Prince George's County Public School abides by that number, neighboring Montgomery County Public Schools extends the graduation requirement to 22 credits.

Institutions	State of Maryland	Montgomery County Public Schools	Prince George's County Public Schools
Subject Areas	Required Credits	Required Credits	Required Credits
English	4	4	4
Mathematics	4	4	4
Science	3	3	3
Social Studies	3	3	3
Fine Arts	1	1	1
Physical Education	0.5	1	0.5
Health Education	0.5	0.5	0.5
Technology Education	1	1	1
Other Electives	4	4.5	4
Total	21	22	21

Table 16: Credit requirements in Maryland (School Year 2016-2017)

Among other requirements, students have to complete a minimum of 75 Student Service Learning Hours (community service) and pass the Maryland High School Assessment Tests or HSA tests in Biology and Government. Additionally students complete the Partnership for Assessment of Readiness for College and Careers (PARCC) tests in both English and Math.

Washington, District of Columbia

In DC Public Schools, students must earn a minimum of 24 credits or Carnegie Units for their high school diploma. Moreover, students are expected to successfully complete 2 College Level or Career Preparatory Courses as determined by their school, and complete 100 hours of community service.

However, schools might impose additional requirements. Columbia Heights Educational Campus (CHEC) requires 28 credits for graduation.

Besides the required 175 hours of community service, each student at CHEC must complete an 80-hour internship in a career field of interest and present a senior portfolio.

Institutions	District of Columbia Public Schools	Ballou High School	Columbia Heights Educational Campus
Subject Areas	Required Credits	Required Credits	Required Credits
English	4	4	6
Mathematics	4	4	5
Science	4	4	4
Social Studies	4	4	4
World Languages	2	2	2
Art	½	½	½
Music	½	0.5	½
Health and Physical Education	1.5	1.5	1.5
Electives	3.5	3.5	4.5
Total	24	24	28

Table 17: Credit requirements in Washington DC (School Year 2016-2017)

Virginia

The State of Virginia requires 22 credits to earn a standard high school diploma. Of the 22 credits, 6 must be verified. When a course is verified, the student has passed the course and its corresponding end-of -course standards of learning (SOL) test, thus meeting the state's high school graduation requirements. Similarly, Fairfax County Public Schools system requires a minimum of 22 credits to confer a standard high school diploma. On one hand, the State requires 3 credits in History and Social Science while Fairfax County Public Schools requires 4 in that core area. Unlike schools in Montgomery County (Maryland), Prince George's County (Maryland), and Washington DC, students attending Fairfax County Public Schools in Virginia must take a course in Economics and Personal Finance to earn their high school diploma.

Institutions	State of Virginia Requirements		Fairfax County Public Schools Requirements	
Subject Areas	Standards Credits	Verified Credits	Standards Credits	Verified Credits
English	4	2	4	2
Mathematics	3	1	3	1
Laboratory Science	3	1	3	1
History & Social Sciences	3	1	4	1
Health & Physical Education	2		2	
Foreign Language, Fine Arts or Career and Technical Ed	2		2	
Economics and Personal Finance	1		1	
Electives	4		3	
Student Selected Test		1		1
Total	22	6	22	6

Table 18: Standard Diploma: Credits requirements in Virginia and Fairfax County (School Year 2016-2017)

Second, students can obtain an Advanced Studies Diploma by earning a minimum of 26 credits, 9 of which are verified.

Institutions	State of Virginia Requirements		Fairfax County Public Schools Requirements	
Subject Areas	Standards Credits	Verified Credits	Standards Credits	Verified Credits
English	4	2	4	2
Mathematics	4	2	4	2
Laboratory Science	4	2	4	2
Historical and Social Sciences	4	2	4	2
World Language/Foreign Languages	3		3	
Health and Physical Education	2		2	
Fine Arts or Career and Technical Ed	1		1	
Economic & Personal Finance	1		1	
Electives	3		3	
Student Elected Test		1		1
Total Credits	26	9	26	9

Table 19: Advanced Studies Diploma: Credits requirements in Virginia and Fairfax County (School Year 2016-2017)

Above all, failure to meet all the expectations could potentially delay the high school student's graduation prospects. School systems generally provide ample notice of changes to graduation requirements. Specifically, graduation requirements can change from one year to the other for the incoming freshman class. Additionally, parents should keep up with the number of credits required for promotion to the next grade.

E. Credit System

African high school students, particularly those from francophone countries, are accustomed to a mark system. The grading scale ranges from zero to twenty (0-20). Simply, school administrators use numbers to assign grades. Thus, the highest grade earned is 20, the average is 10, and 0 is the lowest mark one can get. In the American high school system, each course is assigned a value or a credit. As highlighted in the previous section on graduation requirements, students can earn either half of a credit or one credit per course successfully completed. More often than not, quarter- and semester-long classes earn students half of a credit while yearly courses, such as English or AP courses, earn students one full credit. Again, there is no general rule and parents and students should consult with the school counselor for clarification or peruse the school catalog for course offerings.

F. Instructional Standards

State departments of education provide "standards" or a set of specific guidelines students at each grade level and each subject area should learn in public schools. Put differently, students should demonstrate mastery of explicit skills and competencies at specific stages of their academic career. As objectives, standards drive classroom instruction. Curriculum assessments and state standardized tests serve as tools to measure teacher's accountability in the process. State and school districts disclose content standards. Many times, they are included in the course syllabi handed out either at the beginning of the school year or at the start of a specific course. In some schools, teachers are required to inscribe lesson-related standards on the board. Even more, they might be expected to explain their connection to their daily lesson. There is an ongoing and very contentious debate about the adoption of national standards in education. Without fueling into the controversy of common core standards, parents and students should inquire about the types of standards used at their local school.

G. Teaching Methods

For most people having attended secondary school in Africa, teacher-centered instruction is the norm. In this context, instructors deliver lessons lecture-style to students. In American secondary schools, students experience a variety of teaching styles. Still, they are held to high standards. Some of the most common requirements are direct instruction, inquiry-based learning, cooperative learning, and project-based learning.

Direct instruction

In this model, which is common worldwide, teaching is highly structured and follows strict steps outlined in lesson plans. Students mostly receive and process information provided by instructors through lectures and demonstrations.

Inquiry-based learning

Inquiry-based learning is a complement to direct instruction, and is more student-focused. In this model, students receive research questions or real-life problems that they first investigate, and then attempt to solve by applying previously acquired knowledge. In their quest for solutions, students have the flexibility to use a variety of modalities including technology.

Cooperative learning

Students gather in small groups based on specific criteria and are exposed to a variety of activities designed to facilitate their understanding and mastery of skills taught. Team members assume specific roles within the group, and each participant's input is invaluable for the group's performance and success.

Project-based learning

Students follow various steps and at times work across different subject areas, and have weeks or months to work on specific projects. They present their results to an audience and highlight some of the challenges they encountered in the problem-solving process. Furthermore, they develop skills used in the professional work such as team work and collaboration.

Educators tend to design their courses blending as many of these approaches and learning styles as possible, not only to improve the academic skill set of the students, but at the same time to instill a love for learning in their students. Some courses are designed with specific teaching strategies in mind.

H. Assessments

Usually, teachers assess students' learning via formative and summative assessments. Both allow the educator to measure the progress of their students in the mastery of skills taught and the impact of their teaching style.

Formative assessments

Formative assessments designate all types of assessments given to students to improve their learning. On one hand, they help teachers evaluate the quality of their teaching while on the other, they allow students to acknowledge their strengths and focus on areas where they need improvement. At the end of the process, the feedback resulting from the formative assessments helps to improve the quality of both teaching and learning. A plethora of assessments falls under this group. Below are some examples.

- *Anecdotal notes*: throughout the lesson, a teacher takes notes on the students' progress. Based on his or her observations, the teacher might revise his or her instruction to meet the students' needs.

- *Discussions*: students' responses to the teacher's questions provide an insight into their learning.
- *Exit slips*: at the end of the lesson, the teacher can ask students to respond in writing to a brief question in order to assess their understanding of the concept taught. Though some students tend to neglect this form of assessment, those who choose not to complete it could, in some cases, affect their grades negatively.
- *Self-assessments/peer-assessments*: students evaluate their personal work or their peers' against a rubric or evaluation criteria provided by the teacher. In this instance, students recognize their own strengths and areas of improvement and learn to provide constructive feedback to others.
- *Presentations*: students improve their presentation and public speaking skills by practicing in front of a classmate, a group of peers, or the entire classroom. Depending upon the assignment, they can use PowerPoint, Prezi or individual whiteboards.
- *Think-pair-share*: in this approach, students interact with each other by sharing information related to the concept taught. In the first stage, think, the teacher asks a question for students to consider. In the second stage, pair, students are paired together to exchange their responses to the question asked. During this give-and-take, students learn from each other and might even modify their initial solutions to the problem at the core of this reflective exercise. In the last stage, share, students present their conclusions to the entire class.

African parents and students should bear in mind that some of these formative assessments are graded and may impact the student's grade in a course. Though these assessments might be a means for teachers to reassess and improve their teaching, it is beneficial for students to complete them.

Summative assessments

Teachers give summative assessments to students at the end of a unit or a course to measure their growth relative to an instructional standard. Results from these evaluations can affect the curriculum and courses offered at a school. Some summative assessments include:

- End of unit or end of chapter test
- Interim assessments
- End of semester test
- State-mandated assessments

Compared to formative assessments, these tests may carry more weight on a student's grade.

I. Grading System: Letter Grade

Letter grades characterize the American school system. They are assigned on a percentage and numeric scale ranging from 0 to 100%. Parents and students should inquire about the range assigned to each letter grade in their school district.

Maryland (Montgomery County and Prince George's County)

Both Montgomery County and Prince George's County public schools share a similar grading policy. In both districts, the failing letter grade is "E."

Montgomery County Public Schools		Prince George's County Public Schools	
Letter Grade	Numeric scale in %	Letter Grade	Numeric scale in %
A	90-100	A	90-100
B	80-89	B	80-89
C	70-79	C	70-79
D	60-69	D	60-69
E	0-59	E	0-59

Table 20: Grading policy in Montgomery and Prince George's County Public Schools (School Year 2016-2017)

Washington District of Columbia and Fairfax County (Virginia)

Fairfax County Public Schools		District of Columbia Public Schools	
Letter Grade	Numeric scale in %	Letter Grade	Numeric scale in %
A	93 – 100	A	93 – 100
A-	90 – 92	A-	90 – 92
B+	87 – 89	B+	87 – 89
B	83 – 86	B	83 – 86
B-	80 – 82	B-	80 – 82
C+	77– 79	C+	77– 79
C	73 – 76	C	73 – 76
C-	70 – 72	C-	70 – 72
D+	67 – 69	D+	67 – 69
D	64 – 66	D	64 – 66
F	63 and below	F	63 and below

Table 21: Grading policy in Washington DC and Fairfax County (Virginia) Public Schools (School Year 2016-2017)

For a student to pass the course and meet the credit requirement for a course, he or she needs to earn a passing grade. There is hardly a substitute for a course.

In high school, a student might earn a credit with a grade of "D" as long as the school district policy allows it. However, college-bound students should remember that in most post-secondary schools, the lowest grade to validate a course is "C." A change in mindset is necessary for those striving to be college ready by the end of their high school career.

J. Grade Point Average (G.P.A)

The Grade Point Average is one of the key word African students and their parents alike would regularly encounter throughout their studies in high school and beyond. Due to its salience in the college admission process and in scholarship eligibility, it is crucial for immigrants newly exposed to the American high school system to understand its intricacies. To begin with, there are two types of GPA: unweighted GPA and weighted GPA.

Unweighted GPA

The *unweighted GPA* represents the average of all final course grades taken by a student based on a 4.0 scale. Some call it the traditional GPA. Every letter grade is awarded quality points.

Grade	Points awarded
A	4
B	3
C	2
D	1
E/F	0

Table 22: Unweighted GPA Scale

Every term, the student's report card reflects not only their grades per course but also their *unweighted GPA*. At the end of the semester and/or the school year, students and parents can see the *cumulative unweighted GPA*. It is the average of all final grades earned by a student in all his or her courses during that timeframe. Parent handbooks or guides provide details on the GPA computation in their child's school district.

Weighted GPA

The *weighted GPA* represents the average of all final courses taken by the student based on a 5.0 scale. Here, some courses receive more weight because of the academic rigor they are associated with. Some of those classes are Honors, Advanced Placement (AP), and International Baccalaureate (IB) classes. Akin to the previous type of GPA, each letter grade is bestowed quality points. Though some school districts might slightly tweak the quality points of their weighted GPAs, the usual points distribution is as follow:

Grade	Points awarded
A	5
B	4
C	3
D	1
E/F	0

Table 23: Weighted GPA Scale

Depending upon the nature of courses taken by students, their report card provides information on both their term *weighted GPA* as well as their *cumulative weighted GPA*. As a reminder, a cumulative GPA summarizes the average GPA for all courses taken and recorded on a student's transcript. Just as an Honors or AP course can boost the GPA, an "E" or "F" can significantly decrease the cumulative GPA and at times jeopardize college choices and/or scholarships eligibility. Therefore, students should take all their courses, core and electives seriously beginning with 9th grade to put the odds on their side when the college application window opens.

Weighted or unweighted GPA: which one is the best?

Some professionals in the education field argue that colleges favor weighted GPA in their college application process more so than the unweighted GPA. According to this viewpoint, rigorous content in Honors, AP and IB courses prepares students for the high expectations set in college. Thus, they view enrollment in these courses as a predictor for success in higher education. Others disagree; they declare that students who are enrolled in these programs are often ill prepared for success. Rather, critics equate enrollment into these courses as a means for high schools to inflate the grades of some students blatantly lacking the necessary skills to undertake college work. A recurrent example is their request that schools disclose the number of students who earn college credit on AP exams against those who sit for the exam. The purpose of this example is to bring forth to immigrant parents and students the controversy surrounding students' enrollment in Honors and AP classes. Though a student might be recommended for such a course, parents should bear in mind that the GPA, be it unweighted or weighted is only a single factor among many that colleges review during the admission process. Ultimately, the decision falls on the families to decide as to what route they want to take. African parents should be aware that if they believe their child is not equipped to be successful in Honors and AP coursework, they should meet with the child's counselor or administrator to have him or her transferred to a course where he or she can be successful. At some schools, counselors like to enroll students from French-speaking countries in AP French courses. Some of those students lack the rigorous and advanced written skills required to succeed in such a course. Parents should be watchful so that enrollment in AP courses does not compromise their child's academic performance. Despite the good intentions of the school staff, the family's word in certain cases supersedes what school administrators believe to be in the best interest of a student. Ultimately weighted or unweighted, students should strive for the highest possible GPA to increase the quality of their college application package.

K. Dual Enrollment (High School and College)

In some instances, students with a strong academic record are encouraged to apply to early college programs. In this case, while still in high school, students (preferably juniors and seniors) are enrolled in a maximum of two college classes per semester at a local community college.

School Districts	Community College
Montgomery County Public Schools	Montgomery College
Prince George's Public Schools	Prince George's Community College
District of Columbia Public Schools	Community College of the District of Columbia
Fairfax County Public Schools	Northern Virginia Community College

Table 24: Community Colleges with Dual Enrollment Programs in the DC Area (School Year 2016-2017)

For the most part, these classes fulfill the general studies requirements of a college freshman. High school students taking college classes must fulfill the same requirements as college students. Parents and student should meet and discuss with the staff at their school in charge of this process. In spite of the availability of scholarships and grants, parents might incur some financial charges when their child is in a dual enrollment program. Unlike high school, college education even at a community college level is not free. Benefits from this program vary from one child to the next. While being exposed to the higher education environment, the student gets a head start on their Associate or Bachelor's degree by earning college credits. Time commitment, hard work, and organizational skills are essential in this instance for the student is still responsible for passing all his or her high school classes to graduate on time.

L. Special Education

Across the United States, the Law recognizes 13 categories of disabilities as listed below:

1. Autism
2. Deaf-blindness
3. Deafness
4. Emotional Disturbance
5. Hearing Impairment
6. Intellectual Disability
7. Multiple Disabilities
8. Orthopedic Impairment
9. Other Health Impairment
10. Specific Learning Disability
11. Speech or Language Impairment
12. Traumatic Brain Injury
13. Visual Impairment

Classroom Setting

Students with special needs can learn in various settings depending on their disabilities. The Law requires instruction for each student in the Least Restrictive Environment (LRE). Settings can take one of three forms:

• In class support

Students with special needs are taught in the general education setting with their peers. They receive support from special education teachers who co-teach with content teachers. In other words, there are two teachers in a classroom: one for the content (English, math, social studies, science, etc.) and a second one to modify the lessons so that they are accessible to students with learning disabilities. Parents and students might be confused about having two teachers in the class. However, there are various successful models of co-teaching. An informed parent with a special needs student can inquire about the strategy adopted by the child's educators. For informational purposes, there are six models of co-teaching which enhance classroom learning.

1. One teaches, one observes: one teacher delivers the lesson while the other observes the students throughout the learning process. Collected observations are used to improve instruction.
2. One teaches, one assists: one teacher delivers the lesson while the second teacher provides assistance to students as needed.
3. Parallel teaching: the teachers divide the class in two groups and they simultaneously teach the same lesson in two different corners of the class.
4. Station teaching: the teachers divide the content in two parts. Each teacher delivers the instruction to the first group and repeats the process for the second group.
5. Alternative teaching: With students divided into two groups, one teacher takes care of the large group and the second teacher works with the smaller group.
6. Team teaching: both teachers work together to deliver the lesson simultaneously. They intervene one after the other throughout the lesson.

• Out of class support

Students meet their special education teacher as needed in a different room for extra support with the content material. Often, after the content teacher delivers the lesson in class, if a student with special needs has trouble with the concept taught, he or she goes to the special education teacher during the rest of class time for further academic assistance. Additionally, during tests and exams, students with special needs report to their special education teachers for their accommodations.

- Specialized environment

In cases where instruction cannot be provided to students with their peers in the general education setting, special needs students are taught in a resource or self-contained room within the school building. This room is designed to accommodate students with disabilities outside of the regular classroom.

Individual Education Plan (IEP)

An IEP is a document that highlights the yearly academic goals for a student with special needs and services he or she will receive to ensure success. It is developed by a team (IEP team) made of the parent, child's advocate, teachers, case manager, service providers, and the Local Education Agency (LEA) representative. It must be updated at least once per academic year. In addition, the IEP team can reconvene if further amendments are necessary or if the situation warrants it. The format of the document might vary from one school district to another. The bottom line is that this document is legally binding. Failure to implement its content might result in litigation against the school and/or the school district.

Accommodations

Students with disabilities have trouble processing information and learning content materials. To alleviate that impediment, they receive specific accommodations. Accommodations are changes made to facilitate students' access to information and demonstrate their academic performance on the subject taught. The IEP team considers them during the creation of the student's IEP. Some of the examples include:

- Allowance of adaptive equipment such as tape recorders, word processors, computers, calculators, speech to print technology
- Assignments segmented in different parts to facilitate completion

- Assistance with organization and planning of classwork and/or homework
- Audio books
- Credit for class participation, effort and attendance
- Extra time on assignments, tests and examinations
- Frequent breaks
- Grade only on completed classwork
- Handouts from lessons
- Highlighted textbooks
- Large print material
- Note takers or use of copy paper
- Presentation of material in small steps
- Reader for tests and examinations
- Scaffold/graphic organizers for essay writing
- Supplemental aids (vocabulary, multiplication cards, etc.)
- Study sheets/summary sheets/outlines of most important facts
- Testing in a separate, quieter location
- Testing on several days
- Testing at the best time of the day for the student

Service providers

Depending upon their needs, students with disabilities can work with one or more of the following service providers at their school.

- Audiologist
- Nurse
- Physical therapist
- Psychologist
- Occupational therapist
- Social worker
- Speech pathologist

The list of service providers is not exhaustive but parents should be aware that all services are free of charge.

Exit

Under certain circumstances, a student can exit special education services. The decision should be considered carefully during an IEP meeting. In high school, students receiving special education services as well as parents or legal guardians can request an exit from the program. They both should consult the case manager about the appropriate procedure and the re-admission process should the student's academic performance decline dramatically afterwards.

M. English Language Learners (ELL) or English for Speakers for Other Languages (ESOL)

English language learners take specific courses to improve their skills. Educators use the World-class Instructional Design and Assessment (WIDA) to assess the student's mastery of the English language. The test is divided into four sections: reading, writing, listening, and speaking. For the convenience of parents and students, here is an explanation of the proficiency levels.

Proficiency levels	Description of English Language Proficiency Levels
Level 1: Entering	The student knows and uses minimal social language and minimal academic language with visual support.
Level 2: Emerging	The student knows and uses social English and general academic language with visual support.
Level 3: Developing	The student knows and uses social English and some academic language with visual support.
Level 4: Expanding	The student knows and uses social English and some technical academic language.
Level 5: Bridging	The student knows and uses social and academic language working with grade level material.
Level 6: Reaching	The student knows and uses social and academic language at the highest level measured by the WIDA assessment test.

Table 25: English Language Learners Proficiency Levels
(School Year 2015-2016)

N. Resources for Academic Success

Students who have failed a class receive opportunities to make up for that mishap. In general, students take repeated classes after school. In DC Public Schools, such classes fall under the Credit Recovery Program. In neighboring Montgomery County Public Schools (Maryland), they are known as High School Plus. Some schools might offer those classes online. Therefore, a student needs to secure a computer with Internet access or stay in the school's computer lab to complete the required ckasswork. Other times, a class might be offered at a different campus. It is the student's responsibility to report to that location in a timely manner if he or she has consented to attend that class.

Besides, numerous tutoring opportunities are available to students. Some teachers stay after school for that sole purpose. Community organizations, university programs, and volunteer organizations also provide on-campus tutoring to students after school. The sessions end up early enough allowing students to catch the activities bus back home. Regulations for this late bus might be school-specific. Students might need a pass from a teacher, tutor, coach, or an after-school activity coordinator to board the bus. In Montgomery County Public Schools, Saturday school is another option students can take advantage of to improve their grades. Depending upon the format, students might get help with classwork they struggle with, test preparation, or reinforcement of some difficult concepts. Registration and small fee might be mandatory to attend.

O. Transcript Clean-Up

In some school districts, students can get their high-school transcript "cleaned up." A student who is unhappy about a grade can request to retake a course with the goal of earning a higher grade. Once that occurs, the previous grade is deleted from the student's transcript and replaced by the higher grade. For instance, let's say a student named John earned a D in a class. Unsatisfied with the grade, John applies and is approved for a transcript clean up. He retakes the same class and this time around earns a B. The new and higher grade, B, is recorded on his transcript and the D is removed. Consequently, the higher grade will boost his *cumulative GPA* and paint a better picture of his academic progress. It is worth emphasizing that this action is not available in all school districts. Furthermore, if a student changes school district, the policy might even be more difficult to implement. Equally important is the fact that students generally have full schedules until their senior year where a small number has free periods. In that case, they might not have the luxury to "clean up" their transcript. First-time enrollees, and not repeaters, are given priority during the registration process. The morale in this section is simple. Students must apply themselves from their first day in 9th grade because their *cumulative GPA* can compromise their college options.

By Stéphanie Mbella

Takeaways from Chapter 2

This chapter provides a snapshot of the American high school structure. Salient information for parents and students is highlighted below.

- A high school diploma culminates the end of secondary education in the United States. Some students with severe disabilities earn certificates of attendance or completion.
- Across a school district, numerous career pathways are available.
- Students must meet state, school district, and local school requirements in order to graduate from high school.
- The grading system is a letter grade with the GPA considered a strong indicator of a student's performance and academic potential.
- Dual enrollment is available for students who excel in their studies. However, parents might have to pay for some of the college fees associated with attending a higher education institution.
- Special education provision is the law. Students with special needs are entitled to the best education possible in the least restrictive environment as mandated by their IEP (Individual Education Plan). In some cases, exit from special education could be an option to consider.
- Non-American English native speakers must complete specific English courses to facilitate their language acquisition process. They might get accommodations on exams if warranted.
- Students can participate in tutoring, after school classes, or Saturday School to improve their grades.
- Some students use transcript cleanup processes to delete poor grades from their academic records. However, the process is complicated, arduous, and not available at all schools. Students are better off taking their studies seriously from 9th grade.

Parent and Student Worksheet – Chapter 2

Please complete together as a pair.

Key points	Available options
Types of Degree	☐ International Baccalaureate ☐ High School Diploma ☐ Certificate of attendance ☐ Certificate of completion
School Pathways Considered or Currently Enrolled in	
Magnet Programs Considered or Currently Enrolled in	
Graduation Requirements	Credits Needed: _____ Community Service Hours: _____ State Mandated Tests and Grade
Grade Point Average	Unweighted Cumulative GPA _____ Weighted Cumulative GPA _____
Dual Enrollment in College	☐ Montgomery College ☐ Prince George Community College ☐ Northern Virginia Community College ☐ University of the District of Columbia Community College
Special Education ☐ Yes ☐ No If yes, please check all that apply	☐ Autism ☐ Deaf-blindness ☐ Deafness ☐ Emotional Disturbance ☐ Hearing Impairment ☐ Intellectual Disability ☐ Multiple Disabilities ☐ Orthopedic Impairment ☐ Other Health Impairment ☐ Specific Learning Disability ☐ Speech Impairment ☐ Traumatic Brain Injury ☐ Visual Impairment
English Language Learner ☐ Yes ☐ No	If yes, check proficiency level: ☐ 1 ☐ 2 ☐ 3 ☐ 4 ☐ 5 ☐ 6 ☐Exit
Academic Resources Utilized	☐ Lunch tutoring ☐ After school tutoring ☐ Saturday School

Name: _____ Grade: _____

Student Only Worksheet - Chapter 2

Questions	Answers
How many credits have you earned so far towards your high school diploma?	_____ _____
Are you enrolled in a specific program or academy at your school?	☐ Yes ☐ No If yes, please list some of their completion requirements. _____ _____ _____ _____ _____ _____
In what assessments (formative and summative) do you perform best? Why?	_____ _____ _____ _____
Are you in a dual enrollment program?	☐ Yes ☐ No If yes, please list your dual enrollment courses for the current academic year. _____ _____ _____ _____ _____ _____
If you are a student with special needs, what accommodations work best for you? Why?	_____ _____ _____ _____
If you are an ELL/ESOL student what accommodations work best for you? Why?	_____ _____ _____ _____
How often do you use your school-based academic resources?	☐ Daily ☐ Weekly ☐ Monthly ☐ Never

Chapter 3

College Planning Process

Depending upon whom you talk with, college planning evokes a wide range of emotions. For the uninformed and procrastinators, it can be a daunting task. For the proactive individuals, it can be exciting and an opportunity for bonding between parent and child. Familiarity with the process and following a timeline in many ways create conditions for a smooth college planning. This chapter examines some of the elements of the college planning process. The goal is to empower parents and students about the decisions they would have to take in order to make the whole college planning experience successful.

A. Exposure to the college environment

College fairs

One cannot talk about going to college without taking the time to research or visit at least one. Part of the college planning process includes attendance at college fairs. For 11th and 12th grade students, schools offer at least two college fairs in an academic year, one in the fall and one in the spring. With very few exceptions, college fairs are free. Parents and students are encouraged to attend as many as possible, ask questions to college recruiters about their school, and collect their business cards. Down the road, following up would be easier if a student is interested in applying to a specific college or university after he or she has spoken with a school representative at a fair. At those events, colleges/universities provide brochures about their institutions. This is a great opportunity for parents and students to inquire about the application and admission process, cost of tuition, institutional scholarships, application fee waivers available to students, housing options, the academic resources available to students, and student life on campus. The National Association of College Admission Counseling (NACAC) Fair is one of the most widely publicized college fair in the DMV area. Additionally, community and faith-based organizations sponsor many Historically Black Colleges and Universities (HBCU) or Hispanic College Fairs. Some might offer opportunities to graduating seniors to interview on the spot with prospective college representatives. Students should complete college application packages prior to the day of the college fair to facilitate the review by the college representative. Occasionally, colleges and universities offer full scholarships to strong applicants following their meeting with college representatives at such events.

College tours

College tours represent an additional opportunity to gain knowledge about college life. High schools or various institutions and community organizations can organize them. The diversity of its format provides students with more opportunities to acquire an on-campus experience. Daily, weekend, or summer college tours might include visit of classes, labs, libraries, cafeteria, residential halls, and other amenities colleges offer to their student body. Fly-ins or sponsored overnight tours to some colleges might be selective and only opened to students with strong academic record. Parents can also schedule individual campus tours with their child to get a feel of the academic community of interest to the student.

College open houses

Colleges open their doors to the public for a visit. The format varies depending upon the school. Open houses can require RSVP of attendees or not. Similar to college tours, students and parents get the opportunity to visit the facilities but also interact with the institution staff. This is another great opportunity for students to check schools before they make a final selection as to which college or university they would attend after high school. Exceptionally, some schools might offer onsite admissions to graduating seniors at such events. Students must RSVP for the interview, prepare their application packages, and wear a professional attire.

B. Academics

The student academic record is the basis of college planning. The rigor of academic content (Honors, AP, IB classes, and dual enrollment) and final course grades affect the GPA, which remains a key factor in the college admission process. As mentioned previously, over the course of their studies, students accumulate both unweighted and weighted GPAs, both of which are based on final grades received in each of their classes. Regardless of the nature of the GPA on their transcript, every student should strive for the highest possible. It is worth emphasizing to students as early as the 9th grade that every grade earned affects their college plans. To remain a competitive candidate for colleges and universities, it is in their best interest to maintain as a minimum a solid GPA of "B".

C. Extra-Curricular Activities

Students are encouraged to be actively involved in their school community. Membership to various clubs, sports teams, and volunteering at school events are some examples of school participation. Furthermore, students are expected to give back to society by completing community service hours. The type of the community service, the time commitment, and the student's role in the organization represent some of the factors distinguishing the quality of community service among prospective college applicants. Students should seek active and leadership roles in community service opportunities. Last but not the least, internships offer great opportunities for students to be exposed to a professional environment, acquire marketable skills, and explore some future careers. Many students in high school, particularly seniors work after school. Such experience grants them with the opportunity to delve into the working world and gain an understanding of its dynamics and the expectations placed on employees.

D. Standardized Testing

SAT and ACT

College-bound students must take standardized tests to assess their college readiness. Scores from those tests are one of the factors colleges review in the admission process. Most American universities and colleges accept the Scholastic Assessment Test (SAT) and the American College Test (ACT) as part of their admission process. Briefly, the SAT is a critical reasoning test while the ACT is an achievement test. In other words, the former focuses on critical thinking skills while the latter assesses the content knowledge acquired by a student throughout his or her academic career. In some instances, specific programs within some college might require that prospective candidates submit SAT Subject Test Scores. Students should familiarize themselves with the admission policies of their major of interest. Starting in the academic year 2017-2018, the SAT test would be offered in August and no longer in January. Though the essay portion of each standardized test is optional, students are strongly encouraged to take the test with the essay as some colleges and universities do not consider scores without the essay. Howard University (Washington DC), University of Maryland Baltimore County (Maryland) require the essay scores while Randolph-Macon College and Virginia Union University both in Virginia recommend the prospective freshmen to submit those scores. Equally in the next academic year, the ACT would provide accommodations to eligible and approved English Language Learners. Examples include: a bilingual glossary, instructions in the student's native language and additional time.

SAT	Descriptor	ACT
3 tests and 1 optional essay		4 tests and 1 optional essay
Reading:		English:
52 questions – 65 minutes		75 questions – 45 minutes
Writing and Language:	Format and time	Mathematics:
44 questions – 35 minutes		60 questions – 60 minutes
Mathematics:		Reading:
58 questions – 80 minutes		40 questions – 35 minutes
		Science:
		40 questions – 35 minutes
		Writing: 1 prompt – 40 minutes
Total: 154 Questions		Total: 215 Questions
Common math formulas provided	Test Aid	No formulas provided
1 minute, 10 seconds	Time per question	49 seconds
3 hours	Testing Time	2 hours 55 minutes
+ 50 minutes essay (optional)		+ 40 minutes essay (optional)
7 times an academic year	Scheduling	6 times an academic year
(August, October, November, December,		(September, October, December, February,
March, May, June,)		April, and June)
About 4 weeks before the test	Registration deadlines	About 5 weeks before the test
Late registration fee applies		Late registration fee applies
$54.50 ($43 without essay) *	Cost	$56.50 ($39.50 without essay) *7
Yes but late fee applies	Late registration	Yes but late fee applies
Yes	Test Fee Waivers	Yes
Combined score: 400-1600		Composite score: 1-36
Evidence-based Reading & Writing:		English: 1-36; Reading: 1-36
200-800		
Mathematics: 200-800		Math: 1-36; Science: 1-36
No penalty for incorrect answers	Scoring	No penalty for incorrect answers
Essay (not included in combined score)		Essay (not included in composite score)
Score on 3 dimensions: Reading, Writing,		
and Analysis (score of 2-8 for each		
dimension)		
Almost all US Colleges and Universities	College Acceptance	Almost all US Colleges and Universities
The student sends his or her best scores to	Submission to Colleges	The student sends his or her best scores to
colleges of interest		colleges of interest
https://www.collegeboard.org	Test Administrator	http://www.actstudent.org/

Table 26: Comparative table SAT and ACT
(Source: College Board and ACT)

- **What test to prepare for?**

Sometimes, students are administered both a practice SAT exam or a practice ACT exam and recommended for a prep based on their results. Specifically, students who have a higher score on the PSAT would be steered towards the SAT Prep and students who earned a higher grade on the practice ACT are encouraged to prepare for the ACT test. However, parents and students alike should understand that these are just suggestions. The final decision rests upon the family. Some students recommended to prepare for the SAT have voiced their preference for the ACT and vice-versa. Other students have prepared for both tests because at the end of the day, students send their best scores for consideration to the admission committee of the college they would like to attend. The bottom-line is students' commitment towards their studies.

- **How to sign up for test prep classes?**

In some high schools, standardized test prep is included as an elective in the curriculum. In others, students attend prep sessions at specific times during lunch or after school to preserve their instructional time. Unfortunately, some high schools offer neither option. Thus, students and parents should investigate organizations that offer SAT or ACT prep in their community.

o   In the community

SAT Prep and ACT Prep are large money generators in the United States. Prep sessions are very expensive regardless of the location. In the DMV area, a simple classroom prep course may cost as much as $700. Commonly offered in private sessions, groups average 5 to 20 students. Tutoring hours vary and so is the length of the prep. The content covered might include test preparation strategies and a review of study guide materials. Regardless of their approach, parents should keep in mind that private companies providing this service are businesses seeking to maximize their investment. The more students sign up for their prep, the more money they make. Unfortunately, as in any business venture, the field attracts some unscrupulous individuals who would not hesitate to take advantage of others by deceiving about the quality of their test preparation. If additional services such as personal coaching, personal tutor, online services, and practice tests are provided, the tab for the test prep can go well beyond $3,000. Therefore, parents should not be afraid to request the credentials of the SAT Prep or ACT Prep staff working with their child. Even in cases when the prep is free of charge for students (i.e. community organizations), it would be helpful to know the academic or professional background of the adult who is tutoring your child for the prep. There have been times when there is incompatibility between volunteers' skills and test prep teaching skills. In such circumstances, the student doesn't reap the benefits of the prep.

o   Individual help

Depending on need, learning style, and personality, group SAT Prep or ACT Prep sessions are not suitable for all students. In some instances, all a student needs is the study guide, a timeline to review the prep materials, and a personal tutor. There is an erroneous assumption that private tutoring for test prep is much more expensive than group tutoring. Depending upon the location, an hour of prep can go from $30 to more than $150. This option can be more affordable and cost effective for some parents with a plan as they can negotiate the price with the tutor based on their qualifications and experience. Here is one scenario among many to illustrate. First, the parents purchase one of the test prep guides on the market. Second, they hire an SAT or ACT tutor at a local college. Senior undergraduates and graduate students can be very good candidates for the purpose. Local libraries are ideal meeting locations. Parent and student can interview the prospective tutor and arrange for the terms of their professional relationship. Parents should establish a timeline of tasks or chapters for the tutor and child to cover in the study guide and hold them accountable for meeting those deadlines. Tutors are paid at the end of their sessions. As a takeaway from the test prep section, students should maximize their prep time with regular attendance at their sessions.

o   Online options

The College Board has partnered with the Khan Academy[1] to offer SAT test prep to students who sign up with their organization. In addition, students can use their public library electronic resources to access various databases offering SAT or ACT prep and even other prep materials to future test takers.

- **When to take the SAT or ACT?**

After the PSAT stage in grades nine through 11, college-bound students wonder about the best timing to take the test. Students must consider multiple factors before officially taking either the SAT or the ACT test. At minimum, they should have successfully completed Algebra 2 to give them a foundation for the math portion of the test. College-bound students should take the test at least once during their junior year, preferably in the spring. If they are not satisfied with their scores, they can retake the test as seniors and improve their performance. All students must studiously prep for the exam to maximize their chances of earning the highest possible scores. As a reminder, students select and send on their own volition the scores they would like colleges to consider as a part of their college application materials. Given that there is approximately a three-week turnaround time for students to receive their official test scores, seniors considering early application/decision (November 1st) schools should take the SAT in August and the ACT in September of their senior year to have them available for review with their application materials. Students eligible for fee waivers must plan to use them wisely so that if they exhaust their waivers, they are prepared to pay out of pocket for future standardized tests.

---

[1]   https://www.khanacademy.org/test-prep/sat

- SAT Test and ACT Test Optional

Increasingly, some college and universities are abandoning SAT or ACT scores as a requirement of their admission application. Parents and students can find an updated list with the FairTest of the National Center for Fair and Open Testing.[2] Some schools might provide the option to applicants not to submit their standardized tests scores for consideration by the admission committee if they have a certain GPA. Students and parents should be aware that though SAT or ACT scores might be waived as a part of the application package, they might become very important in the allocation of merit aid among competitive applicants. To put it another way, if students choose not to send their scores to a prospective school, doing so might remove them from consideration for scholarships based on academic performance.

Accuplacer

Upon completion of high school, some students plan to attend a Community College for two years and transfer to a university for their Bachelor's degree. One of the tools community colleges use to assess the college readiness level is by administering the Accuplacer test of College Board. This test assesses the student's competencies in reading, math, and writing. It contains a version for English Language Learners or students whose primary language is not American English. Scores from the Accuplacer test determine which college level courses high school graduates should first take once admitted into the community college. The Accuplacer Test is administered at Montgomery College and Prince George's Community College in Maryland, the Community College of the University of the District of Columbia in Washington DC, and the Northern Virginia Community College in Virginia.

---

[2]   http://www.fairtest.org/university/optional/state

Test of English as Foreign Language (TOEFL)

Non-Native English speakers planning to attend a 4-year college (University) might be required to take the TOEFL to demonstrate their mastery of the English Language prior to their enrollment in courses. Local public libraries usually carry a great selection of preparation materials for students who need to meet this requirement. Students eligible for testing accommodations should request them during the test registration process with Educational Testing Service (ETS) the organization that administers the TOEFL exam.

Importance of standardized testing

It is not uncommon for students to question the significance of standardized testing for their future academic endeavors. High SAT or ACT scores can be on one hand a direct gateway to college level courses. Sometimes, colleges and universities exempt students with college-ready scores in either SAT or ACT from placement tests prior to their enrollment. Students who don't have to take development or remedial courses save time and money. Secondly, high standardized test scores can make a student eligible for merit scholarships, some of which are renewable. Combined with others, they can enable a student to earn a Bachelor's degree without having to incur student loans debt to finance their education. Regardless of the controversy surrounding standardized testing and its ability to predict the likelihood of success in college, they remain a potent college application requirement for high school students.

D. Additional Elements of a College Application Package

In addition to academics, extra-curricular activities, and scores on standardized test, colleges examine the qualitative community service record of their applicants, work and/or volunteer experience. Furthermore, the essay, either a personal statement or one from a specific prompt, recommendation letters from counselor, teachers, and other adults can further strengthen an applicant's package. Once again, colleges review application materials holistically. On September 30, 2016, the University of Maryland College Park organized a Counselor Conference during which an admission representative declared that this institution has 26 factors that the application reviewers use to make an admission decision.

- High school achievement
- Grades in academic subjects
- Progression of performance
- Rank in class (actual or percentile)
- Written expression of ideas (essays)
- Gender
- SAT I or ACT Scores
- Work Experience
- Extenuating circumstances
- Recognition of special event
- Socio-economic background
- Breadth of life experiences
- Extracurricular activities
- Special talents and skills
- Community involvement
- Community service
- Demonstrated leadership
- Academic endeavors outside of the classroom
- Quality of coursework
- Residency status
- Race
- Ethnicity
- Family educational background
- Learning differences
- English as a second language/ language spoken at home
- Geographic origin

Empowered by this new knowledge, it is up to each student, starting from the 9th grade to work hard to stand out among a wide pool of applicants.

Takeaways from Chapter 3

- College planning is equally a behavioral process and this chapter introduces some of its key points. Parents and students are partners in the college planning process.
- Students should have some exposure to the college environment prior to the senior year.
- All high school grades starting from 9th grade influence the college application process.
- Participation in extra-curricular activities constitutes another variable considered in the college application package.
- High SAT and ACT scores increase the odds of acceptance in selective colleges and programs of study. Students have the option to take either test.
- Due to the high cost of test prep, parents should choose the option that best fits within their budget.
- Students should supplement regular attendance at a prep session with personal study time.
- Some universities and colleges are no longer requiring standardized test scores with their college application package. Parents and students should check the updated list of these institutions for further information.
- Unless they have earned a college ready score on the SAT or ACT, community-college bound students would be required to take the Accuplacer placement test to determine their college readiness. This test also has a version tailored for speakers of other languages than English.
- Non-native speakers of American English might be required to take the TOEFL prior to course registration at a university.

Student Only Worksheet - Chapter 3

Answer the following questions to see where you stand compared to the other pool of applicants.

What Do Colleges Want?	Self- Reflection	What would you do to stand out among other applicants this year?
Challenging High School Curriculum ☐ Honors Classes ☐ AP Classes ☐ IB Classes ☐ College Classes	What rigorous classes have you taken?	
Strong G.P.A.	How would you rate your grades since 9th grade? (increasing, decreasing, constant)	
High standardized test scores	Did you earn college-ready scores on the SAT and/or ACT?	
A record of Community Services	What volunteering experiences did you have during which you made a difference in someone's life?	
Work or internship experience	What professional experience do you have?	
Quality involvement in activities	What leadership role have you held at school, in a community organization, or at work?	
Awards earned in High School	What awards have you ever earned in High School? (Honor roll, leadership, athletic, community, etc.)	
A well written essay	How would you characterize your writing skills? (Excellent? Good? Acceptable? Low?) Why?	
Positive recommendations from school staff and/or community members	If asked today, who are the three people at your school and/or in your community who would give you great recommendation letters for a college application?	

Source: Unknown author (2009). Top 10 things colleges look for in a high school student. Retrieved from: http://school.familyeducation.com/collegeprep/high-school/56210.html

Parent Only Worksheet - Chapter 3

Questions	Available options
Have you been to a college tour with your child?	☐ Yes ☐ No
Have you been to a college fair with your child?	☐ Yes ☐ No
Would you be willing to explore and attend universities open houses around your city with your child?	☐ Yes ☐ No
Are you familiar with your child's current GPA?	☐ Yes ☐ No
Is your child involved in extra-curricular activities at school or in the community?	☐ Yes ☐ No
Given your budget, would you be able to afford private test prep sessions for your child?	☐ Yes ☐ No
Is your child eligible for a test fee waiver for the SAT and/or the ACT?	☐ Yes ☐ No
Would you prefer your child only considers SAT/ACT optional schools to reduce the cost of the prep?	☐ Yes ☐ No
If your child has taken a standardized test, did he or she earn college ready scores?	☐ Yes ☐ No
Would your child need to take the ESL Accuplacer Test for non-American English Speakers?	☐ Yes ☐ No
Would your child need to take the TOEFL should they go to a university?	☐ Yes ☐ No

Provide your action plan below for any question answered "no" in the previous table.

_____

_____

_____

_____

_____

_____

_____

_____

Parent and Student College Planning
Worksheet - Chapter 3

Please complete together to assess your child's college planning process.

Key Points	Available Options		
Grade level	☐ 9th ☐ 10th ☐ 11th ☐ 12th		
Academics	Current unweighted GPA: _____ Current weighted GPA: _____		
	Honors classes taken	AP classes taken	IB classes taken
	_____	_____	_____
	_____	_____	_____
	_____	_____	_____
	_____	_____	_____
	_____	_____	_____
	_____	_____	_____
	_____	_____	_____
Extra-curricular activities starting from 9th Grade	Activity	Role/Position	Leadership Position
	_____	_____	☐ Yes ☐ No
	_____	_____	☐ Yes ☐ No
	_____	_____	☐ Yes ☐ No
	_____	_____	☐ Yes ☐ No
	_____	_____	☐ Yes ☐ No
	_____	_____	☐ Yes ☐ No
	_____	_____	☐ Yes ☐ No
	_____	_____	☐ Yes ☐ No
Exposition to college environment (List events attended and/or schools visited)	College fairs	College tours	Open houses
	_____	_____	_____
	_____	_____	_____
	_____	_____	_____
	_____	_____	_____

Standardized test preparation	SAT Test		
	Test Date	Grade	College level scores
	_____	_____	☐ Yes ☐ No
	_____	_____	☐ Yes ☐ No
	_____	_____	☐ Yes ☐ No
	_____	_____	☐ Yes ☐ No
	ACT Test		
	Test Date	Grade	College level scores
	_____	_____	☐ Yes ☐ No
	_____	_____	☐ Yes ☐ No
	_____	_____	☐ Yes ☐ No
	_____	_____	☐ Yes ☐ No

Chapter 4

College Selection Process

Before delving into the college selection process per se, it is important for immigrant parents and students to be aware of the types of institutions of higher education available to graduates.

A. Institutions of Higher Education

Tertiary institutions in the United States can be public or private, and at times religiously affiliated. In general, they fall within three broad groups:

o   4 year colleges (Universities)
o   2 year colleges (Community Colleges or Junior Colleges)
o   Career schools (Technical, trade or vocational schools)

B. Average Graduation Time

For planning purposes, it is important to know the average graduation time based on the type of post-secondary institution and the enrollment status as a full-time or part-time student. The figures captured in the following table represent averages for students attending school full time without interruption. Most importantly, from the beginning, they are college-ready meaning that upon high school graduation, these students do not have to take remedial or development courses to bridge their skill gap in reading, writing, or mathematics.

Program or degree	Awarding institutions	Average graduation time
Career, technical, trade or vocational courses	Career, technical, vocational, and trade school	1-2 years
Associate Degree	Community and Junior Colleges	2 years
Bachelor's Degree	Four year colleges and universities	4 years
Master's Degree	Universities	5-6 years
Doctorate Degree	Universities	7-8 years

Table 27: Post-secondary school options with degrees awarded

Students interested in various professional majors such a nursing, law, or medicine would have to take entrance exams prior to starting their studies. Using our example, the required tests are TEAS (nursing in some schools in Maryland), LSAT (Law School), or MCAT (Medical School). Additionally, they would have to pass an exam granting them the right to work within a specific state.

C. College Selection Criteria

Various factors drive one's impetus in choosing a college. For African parents and students, below are some criteria that can facilitate that process.

Location

Throughout this selection process, a student must consider the physical environment they are likely to thrive academically. Some students prefer an urban environment full of various amenities while others yearn for a secluded area void of distraction. Students' preferences should be reflected on the list of colleges they are considering applying to. Transportation should be factored in as well. While urban areas generally dispose of a better transportation network, urban and semi-urban campuses might have shuttles to bus transit areas or train stations. Regardless, students would have to secure some form of transportation in their immediate community.

Size and type of enrollment

Higher education schools vary in sizes. From large, medium, to small, students should express their preference in their college search. Their inclination should extend to the type of enrollment. Some colleges are single-gendered either all female or all male. Most of the times, they accommodate both sexes.

Diversity of the student body

The Washington DC metropolitan area is not only one of the most ethnically diverse in the nation but also in the world. Though some enclaves of homogeneity exist in the community, students graduating from local high schools are accustomed to being in environments reflective of that reality. Some students are more comfortable pursuing their studies in an environment that mirrors their past experiences. If that is the case, they should explore college and universities that meet that personal expectation.

Academic programs and resources

The reputation of a school is one of the most important factors students consider prior to filling out their application. The number of majors offered and the faculty-student ratio come next. Undecided undergraduate students would likely enjoy a school with a broader selection of majors ranging from undergraduate to graduate degrees. Similarly, students benefit from smaller classroom size, which is not always possible in all higher education settings. The presence of libraries endowed with large selections of research databases and laboratories equipped with the latest technology would undoubtedly attract students leaning towards specific majors. Last but not the least, the diversity of support services for students including but not limited to writing, math, and science centers, tutoring, and special accommodations for students with special needs constitute additional factors high schoolers should explore in their college selection process.

By Stéphanie Mbella

Financial cost

College is very expensive. As the student and their parent delve into the selection process, the amount of money they would have to disburse for their child's education is paramount in their decision process. This section dissects some of the items parents should take into consideration as they explore college choices with their child.

- Tuition and fees

For an in-state (resident) student, the most affordable college tuition is an in-state or public college or university. A student who decides to study in an out-of-state public university would have to pay more. As an illustration, Maryland high school graduates desiring to attend Virginia's public universities or colleges would have to pay more and vice-versa. It is worth noting that private schools tend to have the same financial obligations for incoming students regardless of residency status. As examples, McDaniel College, George Washington University, and Shenandoah University apply the same tuition and fees to their students. In a similar vein, though Howard University and Hampton University are designated HBCUs (Historically Black Colleges and Universities) institutions, as private schools, they share a similar policy on tuition and fees. Parents should work with their children to ensure that they select schools that are financially affordable to the family and for which the student' s scholarships would assuage the financial burden of college.

Schools	State	Annual In-State Tuition	Annual Out-of-State Tuition	Annual In-State Fees	Annual Out-of-State Fees	Total In-State	Total Out-of-State
Bowie State University	MD	$4,824	$15,391	$2,147	$2,147	$6,971	$17,538
McDaniel College	MD	$36,960	$36,960	$0	$0	$36,960	$36,960
Salisbury University	MD	$5,912	$14,258	$2,216	$2,216	$8,128	$16,474
University of Maryland College Park	MD	$7,390	$26,576	$1,772	$1,772	$9,162	$28,348

George Washington University	DC	$47,290	$47,290	$53	$53	$47,343	$47,343
Howard University	DC	$21,450	$21,450	$1,233	$1,233	$22,683	$22,683
University of the District of Columbia[8]	DC	$4,518	$8,158	$620	$620	$5,138	$8,778
George Mason University	VA	$7,220	$25,904	$2,688	$2,688	$9,908	$28,592
Hampton University	VA	$18,618	$18,618	$2,106	$2,106	$20,724	$20,724
Shenandoah University	VA	$28,514	$28,514	$1,420	$1,420	$29,934	$29,934
Virginia Tech	VA	$9,619	$24,769	$1,838	$2,442	$11,457	$27,211

Table 28: Resident vs. nonresident tuition and fees -
Estimates from the school year 2013-2014
Source : www.cappex.com

- Room (dormitory) and board (meal plan) for students planning to reside on campus

For the most part, high school graduates relish at the idea of living independently, away from parents their first year of college. Ideally, both student and parent should visit the school before the student commits to attending upon graduation. For many parents, especially African immigrants, it is a challenging. Therefore, it is important for the student to know what types of accommodations they can be comfortable with and thrive in, and for parents to know if they are within the family budget. Certain colleges require freshmen to reside on campus for specific reasons. In such a case, students don't have the luxury to reside off campus whether they are within communiting distance from their primary home. Coupled with that, students would have to purchase a meal plan as not all residence halls, particularly for incoming students provide amenities for meal preparation. Students with particular dietary needs should make sure that their chosen school would be able to accommodate them properly before they commit to attend that school.

Schools	State	In-State Tuition and Fees	Total Out-of-State Tuition and Fees	Room and Board	Books and Supplies	Total Annual In-State Cost	Total Annual Out of State Cost
Bowie State University	MD	$6,971	$17,538	$9,336	$2,200	$18,507	$29,074
McDaniel College	MD	$36,960	$36,960	$8,640	$1,200	$46,800	$46,800
Salisbury University	MD	$8,128	$16,474	$10,240	$1,300	$19,668	$28,014
University of Maryland College Park	MD	$9,162	$28,348	$10,280	$1,130	$20,572	$39,758
George Washington University	DC	$47,343	$47,343	$11,378	$1,275	$59,996	$59,996
Howard University	DC	$22,683	$22,683	$13,460	$3,000	$39,143	$39,143
University of the District of Columbia	DC	$5,138	$8,778	$15,375	$1,200	$21,713	$25,353
George Mason University	VA	$9,908	$28,592	$10,730	$1,120	$21,758	$40,442
Hampton University	VA	$20,724	$20,724	$9,230	$1,100	$31,054	$31,054
Shenandoah University	VA	$29,934	$29,724	$9,564	$1,500	$40,998	$40,788
Virginia Tech	VA	$11,457	$27,211	$8,170	$1,120	$20,747	$36,501

Table 29: Resident vs. nonresident tuition and fees -
Estimates from the school year 2013-2014
Source: www.cappex.com

- Books and supplies

They constitute one of the hidden costs of college. Books are very expensive, and whether students might be able to purchase used books, rent books, or download e-books, they remain an important budget item that is difficult to estimate. It should not come as a surprise for parents to have students disburse a minimum of $500 for books per semester of studies.

Parents should bear in mind that tuition increases every year and the figures herein used might have increased significantly in respective schools.

- Additional costs

Transportation and personal expenses constitute additional costs that should be included in the cost of attendance. Airfare, train or bus transportation, and allowance for personal expenses must be included in the budget as well. Given their fluctuating nature, they are not included in the cost of attendance used for illustration purposes in this section.

- Available financial aid

Some students select schools based on the available financial aid opportunities. Some colleges tend to be generous in that regard with students from low-income families and strong academic record. Students who apply by the first application deadline might be automatically considered for these institutional scholarships. By law, every college receiving federal monies should have a net price calculator to enable parents and students to estimate as accurately as possible the net cost of attending a particular institution. This information is available online on the school's financial aid website or the student can request it from a college representative at a college fair or at an open house. Supplementary aid can be need-based (economic status), merit-based (academic record), or work-study (paid campus job). Some schools offer specialized scholarships for athletes and in various disciplines such as art, music, or science.

- Additional considerations

There are additional considerations students take into account when choosing a college. Safe residence halls or campus housing with accessible laundry facilities, wireless services, and state of the art fitness and health centers are becoming the norm. Study abroad opportunities, clubs, organizations, athletics and intra-mural activities to boost the quality of student life and maximize the college experience all factor in the decision of prospective college students. Career and professional networking opportunities can be very important for some students. After all, college graduates want to land a good job right out of school. The diversity of the student body is paramount for some minority group students. Some African-American students express their preference for a Historically Black College or University (HBCU) while some Latino students favor institutions members of the Hispanic Association of Colleges and Universities (HACU). In the similar vein, religious affiliation, and opportunities to be involved in athletic and extra-curricular activities represent additional factors students tend to examine during their college selection process.

D. Community Colleges

Schools	State	Annual In-State Tuition	Annual Out-of-State Tuition	Annual In-State Fees	Annual Out-of-State Fees	Total In-State	Total Out-of-State
Montgomery College	MD	$6,870	$9,420	$1,794	$2,304	$8,664	$11,724
Prince George's Community College	MD	$4,440	$6,720	$1,130	$1,130	$5,570	$7,850
University of the District of Columbia	DC	$4,518	$8,158	$620	$620	$5,138	$8,778
Northern Virginia Community College	VA	$3,435	$7,737	$242	$674	$3,677	$8,411

Table 30: DC Area Community Colleges Resident vs. nonresident tuition and fees - Estimates from the school year 2013-2014
Source: https://www.cappex.com/

In comparison to four-year schools, community colleges are the most affordable option for the first two years towards a bachelor's degree. These institutions in the DMV area don't have dorms and as such, the housing choice is left to the discretion of each student. It is important to note that the University of the District of Columbia houses both a community college and a four-year school. Parents and student should inquire about the specific institution of interest to them.

For many reasons, there is stigma attached to community colleges. A recurrent one questions the quality of its education. These institutions boast of highly educated faculty, small class size, and multiple academic resources to ensure students' success. As nationally accredited institutions, the credentials of their graduates are acceptable across the United States.

Overall, the cost of attendance at a community college is lower than the cost of attending a four-year college. Students can take the first two years of post-secondary education at a community college, earn an associate's degree, and transfer to a university to earn their bachelor's degree. Their commitment to their studies either at a four- or two-year school paves the way to their success.

Schools	State	In-State Tuition and Fees	Total Out-of-State Tuition and Fees	Room and Board	Books and Supplies	Total Annual In-State Cost	Total Annual Out of State Cost
Montgomery College	MD	$8,664	$11,724	$13,194	$1,200	$23,058	$26,118
Prince George's Community College	MD	$5,570	$7,850	$7,600	$1,500	$14,670	$16,950
University of the District of Columbia	DC	$5,138	$8,778	$15,375	$1,200	$21,713	$25,353
Northern Virginia Community College	VA	$3,677	$8,411	$6,374	$1,700	$11,751	$16,485

Table 31: Community College resident vs. nonresident cost of attendance - Estimates from the school year 2013-2014 [3]
Source : https://www.cappex.com/

In choosing a college, one should bear in mind that for residency purposes, public in-state universities cost less than their out-of-state counterparts. In other words, the tuition would be less for student attending college in their home state than out of state. Some people shy away from

---

3   Transportation and personal expenses are not included in the cost of attendance in this section.

cost-prohibitive schools where they would have to borrow large sums of money to finance their child's education. This situation can be offset by a student earning scholarships money to help cover for the costs of college. The preparation for this process starts at their entrance in 9th grade.

Takeaways from Chapter 4

- College selection is the bedrock of a successful academic experience in higher education. It is a delicate process that can be done in a multitude of ways. However, each parent and college-bound student should consider some elements in their quest for the school that is the best for the student.
    o Location
    o Size
    o Types of enrollment
    o Reputation (number of majors)
    o Academic support (lab and equipment, libraries, writing, math, and science labs)
    o Diversity of student body
    o Tuition and fees
    o Available financial aid
    o Facilities (housing and fitness centers)
    o Student life activities (clubs, organizations, sports)
    o Affiliation (HBCU, HACU, religion)
    o Job prospects after graduation
    o Alumni network
- Universities can be found in all types of environments across the US. That gives students the option to select the institution situated where they would most likely blossom academically. Small, medium, or large size campuses, co-educational or not, students select the school that caters best to their desires.
- It is not uncommon for students to change their majors multiple times during their freshman and sophomore years. This process is easy if they are not enrolled in a professional program such as pre-law or pre-med.
- Undecided students would benefit by enrolling in a school that has two or three majors of interest just in case they change their mind along the way.
- Financially, it is cheaper to attend public institutions in the state of residency than out-of-state and private counterparts. Some

schools have large endowments and a great alumni network. As such, they have the latitude to provide substantial scholarship packages to their incoming freshmen. However, in the age of budget cuts and increasing tuition, it is crucial not to make any assumptions on the generosity of a given school as financial aid packages vary from one year to the next.

- It is always important to check and compare schools that would meet the financial needs of the students. Parent and child might disagree on the choices. At the end of the day, both parties would have to compromise especially if parents would have to take up loans to help pay for the education or if students are undocumented.

Parent Worksheet – Chapter 4

Key Points	Available Options
Select all types of institutions you would like your child to attend.	☐ In-state public school ☐ In-state private school ☐ Out-of-state public school ☐ Religious school ☐ Community College ☐ Out-of-state private school ☐ No preference
Do you have a specific college/university you would like your child to attend? Why or why not?	
In the event your family cannot afford a 4-year college tuition for your child, are you comfortable having the conversation about a community college as a viable option? Explain your answer.	
Based on your family circumstances and your child academic standing select all types of aid he or she might be eligible for?	☐ Need-based ☐ Merit-based ☐ Work study ☐ Athletics ☐ None ☐ I don't know
In the event your child cannot secure on campus housing are you comfortable having them stay with roommates off-campus? Explain your answer.	
Are there any special circumstances likely to affect your child's quality of life on campus? (Health, diet, behaviors, and other important issues)	
If you are a parent of an undocumented student, is the child aware of their legal status in the United States? If yes, list some of the schools to which he or she can apply. If no, how would you share this crucial piece of information with the child?	
Please rate by order of importance to you some of the college selection criteria.	____ Size ____ Available ____ Academic ____ Location Financial Support ____ Student Aid ____ Facilities Life ____ Diversity ____ Reputation ____ Tuition of Student and Fees Body ____ Types of ____ Alumni Enrollment ____ Affiliation ____ Job Prospects

BY STÉPHANIE MBELLA

Name: _____   Grade: _____

Student Worksheet – Chapter 4

Check all criteria you consider in your college selection process

Key Points	Available Options
Types of Colleges of Interest	☐ Public only ☐ Private only ☐ Both types ☐ I don't know
Institutions (Where do you want to attend college?)	☐ 2-year college (Community College or Junior College) ☐ 4-year college (University) ☐ Career school (Technical, Trade, Vocational) _____ *Specify*
Location	☐ In-state only ☐ Out- of- state only ☐ Both
	☐ Metropolitan area ☐ Urban area ☐ Rural area
Academics	☐ Reputation of the school ☐ Number of majors of study ☐ Faculty-student ratio ☐ Library size ☐ Laboratory and equipment ☐ Tutoring centers ☐ Math help centers ☐ Writing center ☐ Lab assistance ☐ Special accommodations
Size and enrollment	☐ Large size campus ☐ Medium size campus ☐ Small size campus
	☐ All female campus ☐ All male campus ☐ Co-educational campus
Financial cost	☐ Tuition and fees ☐ Room and board ☐ Books and supplies
Available aid	☐ Need-based aid ☐ Merit-based aid ☐ Work study
	☐ Specialized scholarships: _____ ☐ R.O.T.C *Specify major*
Other considerations	☐ Athletic activities ☐ Career Center ☐ Diversity of the student body (Ethnic minorities: HBCU / HACU) ☐ Family and friends ☐ Internship opportunities ☐ Religion ☐ Study abroad programs

Chapter 5

College Application Process

Ideally, by the end of their junior year, all students should know the college admission type they will pursue as seniors. Thus, they can begin their college application process early in the summer and produce high quality applications that would enable them to stand out among thousands of applicants.

A. Application Timeline

College-bound students should be aware of four types of college applications: early decision, early action, regular decision, and rolling admission. It is not uncommon for schools to offer between two to three types of admissions per academic year. Early decision, early action, and regular decision are most common for universities and rolling admission for community colleges. Application deadlines might change from one year to the next or they may remain the same. November 1, November 15, December 1, and December 15 constitute some of the earlier deadlines in the fall college application process. For better planning, students must familiarize themselves with the admission deadlines of their prospective colleges as early as in the summer as each comes with its benefits and challenges.

Types	Definition	Benefits	Drawbacks	Suggestions
Early decision	Apply to a college early between mid-October and mid-December	High admission rates Early acceptance, rejection or deferral letter sent out by end January – Mid February Best consideration for institutional scholarships (scholarships given out by the college) Good option for best fit school	Binding (once accepted the student must attend that school and withdraw applications from other schools).	The cost of college should not be an issue for students selecting that option.
Early action/ priority application	Apply to college early between mid-October and mid-December	High admission rates Early acceptance If rejected, a student still has time to apply for regular admission. Best consideration for institutional scholarships (scholarships given out by the college) Students have until the spring to commit to attend that school.	Single choice/restricted early action prevents students from applying for early application to more than one school.	Be very organized and proactive in the application process.
Regular admission	School sets its own date for accepting applications	No restrictions on the number of schools to which a student can apply	Lower admission rates compared to early decision and early action. Admission status in the spring (End of March – April)	Be organized to meet all the application deadlines for all the schools of interest.

| Rolling admission | There is no application deadline. Admissions decisions made in four to eight weeks | Students can apply at any time. | The freshman class might be full but colleges would not disclose that information rather continue to accept applications. Late applicants might not receive the full aid they deserved due to tardiness. | Apply as early as possible to secure a spot. If applying late in the spring or in the summer, contact the admissions office first to ensure that they are still accepting and reviewing applications. |

Table 32: Different types of college admissions

B. Application Format

Currently, students can submit paper or electronic college applications. Schools are moving towards the latter for efficiency purposes and cost-saving measures. Regardless of type, students can access the application in both formats if available on the school website. For the electronic application, students would have to create an account with an ID and password tailored to the specific requirements of the college. It is the students' responsibility to remember the login credentials granting them access to their college applications.

• Common Application

Many US colleges and universities have embraced the Common Application (better known as the Common App) in their admission process. As any tool, this application presents both benefits and limitations. On the pros side, the online process reduces clutter. Additionally, it is a time saver since students complete a single application simultaneously sent to many schools. As such, they can pace themselves and work efficiently. Yet, on the other end, the lack of downloadable form prevents educators from organizing practice workshops for students before they get started on their lengthy application. The general nature of the essay prompts thwarts students from tailoring it to a specific school. Some schools require additional essays and information and each student should ensure proper completion of the application. For the 2016 - 2017 academic year there are six major sections to the application.

Sections	Sub-sections	Detailed information needed
Profile	Personal information	Name, date of birth, gender
	Address	Permanent home address
	Contact details	Email address and phone numbers
	Demographics	Religious affiliation, US army status, ethnicity
	Geography	Country of birth, number of years in the US and/or outside the US
	Language	Number of languages spoken
	Citizenship	US Citizen, Permanent Resident or refugee, non-US citizen, Social Security Number for students applying for FAFSA
	Scholarship information	A new partnership in scholarship matching
	Common App Fee Waiver	Acknowledgement to be a fee waiver recipient
Family	Household	Parents marital status, information on parent 1, parent 2, and siblings
Education	Current or most recent high school	Date of entry at school, graduation date, counselor's information (name, title, phone, email address).
	Community organizations	Name of the organization, name, title, phone, email address of person who provided the assistance in completing the application
	Education interruption	Indicate high school progression including year of interrupted studies if any
	College and universities	Information on previous college coursework (while in high school)
	Grades	GPA (cumulative weighted and cumulative unweighted)
	Current courses	List of all courses taken in the senior year
	Honors	List of academic honors
	Future plans	areer goal and highest college degree desired
Testing	ACT, SAT, AP, IB, TOEFL	Provide detailed scores of test (s) taken
Activities	Extracurricular activities	Arts, athletics, clubs, employment
Writing	Essay	Write an essay based on chosen prompt
	Disciplinary history	Suspension, probation, or suspension (if applicable)
	Additional information	If applicable

Skip logic is an essential characteristic of the Common Application. In simple terms, the computer prompts specific questions to the student based on his or her previous answers. For example, if a student responds to the question about the number of siblings to be 1, he or she would be prompted to provide information for a single individual. If the student instead indicates he or she has 3 siblings, he or she would have to provide the names, age, gender, and educational level of 3 persons.

• Coalition for Access, Affordability, and Success Application

The class of 2017 was introduced to another additional application for college application purposes. Conceptually, it is similar to the common application in the sense that a group of colleges and universities endorses it. Member schools claim financial affordability for admitted students. The student interface is divided in three sections: a profile, a locker, and the colleges.

With the profile, students get to provide information about their personal background, academic performance and coursework, and extra-curricular activities. The University of Maryland College Park is expected to transition exclusively to the Coalition Application for the 2017-2018 school year. The Coalition Application is comprised of three major sections as indicated in the following table.

Sections	Sub-sections	Detailed information needed
Profile	Personal information	Name, gender, date of birth, social security number
	Contact information	Phone, mailing address
	Demographic information	Ethnicity, languages spoken
	Citizenship information	US citizenship, birthplace
	Family information	Parents/guardians: educational level, occupation, address
		Siblings: full names, date of birth, educational level
		Household size
	High School	GPA, rank, class size
	9th – 11th Grades Coursework	List of all classes taken from 9-11 grades
	12th Grade Coursework	List of all classes to be taken in the 12th grade
	College Information	Number of college or dual enrollment credits earned
	College Coursework	For college coursework completed
	Test Scores	Standardized test scores reports (SAT, ACT, IB, AP, TOEFL, AL)
	Financial Aid	Types of fee waivers available to student (Free and Reduced
		Lunch, College Board, ACT, NACAC, TRIO Program)
	Honors and Distinctions	School, local, regional, state, and international
	Academic Interests	List of college majors of interest
	Extra-Curricular Activities	Arts, clubs, organizations, sports, volunteer, work
		All activities per grade and hours of involvement per week and
		brief description
		Leadership position (if any)
Locker	Media	Upload videos
	Official Documents	Transcripts, recommendation letters
Colleges	Select schools of interest	Add all colleges of interest

Given the depth of the information students must report on both the Common Application and the Coalition for Access, Affordability, and Success Application, they should collect the following documents before getting started:

1. Student transcript: list of the completed coursework
2. Resume (listing all extracurricular activities and awards earned in high school)
3. Standardized tests scores: SAT, ACT, and AP, IB, TOEFL
4. Family information: parent (marital status, country of birth, job status, employer)
5. Household information, marital status of each parent, country of birth, job status, and employer
6. Social Security Number (for students planning to apply for FAFSA)

Preferably, students should create their accounts and complete their profiles in the summer prior to the beginning of their senior year, as this process is time consuming.

- School-specific application

Other schools have personalized applications for prospective students. Similar to the Common App, they more or less require the following information:

- Personal and educational data
- Honors and awards
- Extracurricular, personal, and volunteer activities
- Employment, internship, and summer activities
- Disciplinary information
- Essays (long and short)
- Audition or portfolio (if applicable)
- Interview (if applicable)
- Application fee waiver (only for eligible students)

In addition to all of the above, students would have to sign their application to acknowledge the veracity of the information submitted to the admission committee.

Briefly, some of the components of the college application package are as follow:

- Application
- Recommendation letters
  o From counselor
  o From teachers
  o From other recommender (if applicable)
- Standardized scores (ACT or SAT)
  o The student should request the scores be sent from College Board or ACT directly to the colleges.
- Official transcript
  o The student should request official transcripts to be sent to colleges of interest as per school protocol.
- Fee waiver or application fee
- All required supplemental materials
- Mid-year report (first semester grade of senior year if applicable)

C. College Applications Costs

Applying to college is expensive. Eligible students might have limited fee waivers to help with the fees. Not all colleges accept application fee waivers. Thus, parents need to know that in the process, they might have to disburse some money. Application fees can range from $40 to $90 dollars depending upon the school. In spite of the convenience of the Common App i.e. one application for many schools, students are responsible for all application fees. In the first case scenario, the student is applying to six schools, all of which are on the common application. After completing a single application with additional materials, parents would have to pay $360 for all these applications.

Schools	State	Application fee
American University	Washington DC	$70
Johns Hopkins University	Maryland	$70
Old Dominion University	Virginia	$50
The Catholic University of America	Washington DC	$55
University of Maryland Baltimore County	Maryland	$50
Virginia Commonwealth University	Virginia	$ 65
	Total	$360

Table 33: Sample college application fees for Common Application Schools (School Year 2016-2017)

The same applies for non-common app schools as illustrated in the second case scenario below. Here, the total would be $285 since Trinity University waives fees for online applicants.

Schools	State	Application fee
Georgetown University	Washington DC	$75
Liberty University	Virginia	$50
Mount St. Mary's University	Maryland	$45
Towson University	Maryland	$45
Trinity Washington University	Washington DC	Fee waived for online application
University of Virginia	Virginia	$70
	Total	$285

Table 34: Application fees for some Non-Common App Schools (School Year 2016-2017)

- Additional costs of college applications

Besides college application fees per se, parents and students should add the cost of sending transcripts, an essential part of any college application package, to each school to which the student applies. Students might have to disburse money to request their official standardized scores (SAT or ACT) to be sent to colleges of interest. A simple way to save up this money is to list all colleges of interest during the free submission window provided by College Board and ACT after taking a test. Still, some remaining balance might have to be covered. Students eligible for fee waivers might receive some financial assistance with college application fees. For instance, College Board and NACAC offer college applications fee waivers to eligible students.

- Application follow-up

After all materials have been sent, students must check their email for any correspondence from the colleges in case of clarification requests or additional inquiry. The next step would be to complete the Free Application for Federal Student Aid (FAFSA) and other financial documents necessary to ensure the payment of their college education in the following year. Once a student receives an admission letter, he or she would have to confirm his or her decision to attend the school by contacting the admissions office and by giving a specific deposit to secure a spot in the incoming freshman class. The common deadline for school selection is May 1st, known by many as "decision day." Students planning to live on campus might have to provide an additional deposit for housing.

- To how many colleges should a student apply?

During the application process, students and parents inquire about the number of colleges to which the student should apply to ensure that he or she is accepted into a school that is a good fit. In general, students are advised to apply to at least one school in each of the following categories because of the competitiveness in college admissions. Above all, the student should see him- or herself thriving within each of the institutions selected.

1. Reach Schools
   These are schools on the student's list with the highest and most competitive admissions standards. Their reputation constitutes a strong incentive for students' attractiveness. For the best consideration, the student must meet or exceed the minimum requirements of the previous freshman class. Granted, not all top schools advertise their required minimum GPA and SAT or

ACT scores, but college representatives or admission officers can provide the information.

2. Target Schools

   Students can get into these schools if their academic records place them within the average of the recent freshman class. Some students with credentials on the borderline might make the cut on the first round or even be put on the waiting list for later consideration.

3. Safety Schools

   As the name indicates, these are schools where the student's current academic record would most likely grant them admission. Most students consider these schools as back-up plans in case they are not admitted to their target schools.

Applying to schools in either category is a sure way for a student to multiply their chances in the college admission process.

Takeaways from Chapter 5

- There are many options for college application each with its benefits and limitations. Students must select the one that best fits their needs.
- Regardless of the choice, the process is time-consuming and appropriate planning would help relieve the stress.
- Admissions offices at many schools use the common application. Despite its convenience, students are responsible for all college application fees.
- The Coalition for Access, Affordability, and Success Application is another college application option. Students can upload videos to share with prospective colleges.
- Following the school protocol with respect to recommendation letters and transcript requests helps ensure that all application materials are sent to colleges in a timely manner.
- Essays are major components of a college application. Students are strongly encouraged to have someone help with the editing so that they submit the best quality work to colleges.
- Students should maintain good grades even after their admission into a college so that the college doesn't rescind their offer for declining performance.
- The student's college list should contain at least one reach, one target, and one safety school.

Parent and Student Worksheet # 1 – Chapter 5

Please complete together.

Key Points	Available Options		
What college admission types is your child considering?	□ Early Decision □ Regular Admission	□ Early Action □ Rolling Admission	□ Restricted Early Action
Select all information accessible to your child for the college application process	□ Child: social security number □ Parents: dates of birth □ Parents: divorce/separation date □ Parents: employer (s) □ Siblings: dates of birth	□ Child: immigration status □ Parents: educational levels □ Parents: occupations/jobs □ Siblings: full names □ Siblings: educational levels	
Is your child eligible for a fee waiver?	□ Yes	□ No	□ I don't know
If yes, what organization provided the college application fee waivers?			
How many college application fee waivers is your child eligible for?			
Is your child enrolled in a college readiness program?	□ Yes	□ No	□ I don't know
If yes, when was the last time you met as a team?			
When was the last time you had a college planning meeting with your child's counselor?			
Does the school help students pay for AP exams in May?	□ Yes	□ No	□ I don't know

Student Worksheet # 1 – Chapter 5

Complete the following table to estimate the cost of your college applications.

#	Schools	State	School Categories (R, T, S)	Application Types (SA, CA, CAAS)	Admission Types (ED, EA, ERA, RED, ROA)	Application Deadline	Fee
1							
2							
3							
4							
5							
6							
7							
8							
9							
10							
11							
12							
13							
14							
15							
						Total Cost	

Legend

School Categories:

R= Reach School   T= Target School   S= Safety

Application Types:

SA= School App   CA= Common App   CAAS= Coalition App

Admission Types:

ED= Early Decision   EA = Early Action   ERA= Early Restricted Action

RED= Regular Decision   ROA= Rolling Admission

Parent and Student Worksheet # 2 – Chapter 5

Complete the following table to estimate your college application budget.

Items	Fee per Unit	Number of Units	Total Cost
SAT Test (s) with writing			
ACT Test (s) with writing			
AP Test (s)			
College 1 - Application fee			
College 2 - Application fee			
College 3 - Application fee			
College 4 - Application fee			
College 5 - Application fee			
College 6 - Application fee			
College 7 - Application fee			
College 8 - Application fee			
College 9 - Application fee			
College 10 - Application fee			
Submission of SAT Scores to College (s)			
Submission of ACT Scores to College (s)			
Submission of Transcripts to College (s)			
Enrollment Security Deposit			
Housing Security Deposit			
Estimated Budget			

Chapter 6

College Major Selection

As they complete applications, high school students are asked to state their intended major field (s) of study. Not all students are certain what they would like to study in college. Before we examine some of the college selection options, let's begin this section by dispelling some recurrent misconceptions in the African community.

A. Misconceptions

1. You must pick your major directly from high school.

False: Some students select "undecided" as far as a major is concerned on their college application. That's perfectly fine for the admission committee. Once enrolled as a freshman, a student would explore major opportunities with a college academic advisor.

2. All majors are accessible from high school.

False: Some schools have "impacted majors" or "limited enrollment majors," indicating majors where there are more applicants than available seats. The selection is very competitive and applicants might have to meet additional admission requirements or even be on a waiting list for some time prior to their official acceptance into the program.
Examples of impacted/limited enrollment majors:
  (1) University of Maryland College Park (MD): Business and Journalism

(2) University of Maryland Baltimore County (MD): Computer Science and Electrical Engineering

3. Choosing a major and choosing a career are similar.

False: A major is a field of study leading to an occupation or a career
Examples:
(1) A student who majors in Biology can become a Laboratory Technician.
(2) A student who majors in English can become a Journalist.
(3) A student who majors in Mathematics can become an IT Systems Administrator.

4. You can only choose one major in college.

False: Colleges provide the opportunity to students to have a double major or a major and a minor.
Examples:
(1) A student can major in International Relations and Psychology. In this scenario, the student would earn two degrees: a Bachelor's in International Relations and another Bachelor's in Psychology.
(2) A student can major in Business and have a minor in Economics. In this scenario, the student would earn a Bachelor's in Business but would have a strong understanding of Economics.

5. A major and a career are for life.

False: People have various careers throughout their lives and it is not uncommon for them to return to school and major in a new field of interest.

B. How to Choose a College Major?

There is a multitude of ways to select a college major. This guide highlights four i.e. interests, skills, values, and personality.

1. Interests

In this case, major selection focuses on things one loves doing. One of the most common method used in educational settings and that students and parents can explore on their own is the Holland personality codes. According to Dr. John Holland who devised this theory, people can fall under six categories of occupations:

- Realistic
- Investigative
- Artistic

- Social
- Enterprising
- Conventional

The short acronym of this approach is RIASEC. Holland codes can be used to explore potential college majors. During the college selection process, educators encourage students to complete a Holland Code career assessment to provide them with an overview of career clusters based on interests. Some tests are available online for free and the results allow the student to explore the breath of careers deriving from a specific major. Generally, RIASEC personality tests use Likert-style questions with students rating different tasks from the most enjoyable to the least enjoyable. After securing a list of careers from a RIASEC test, students can examine their future job outlook. There are jobs that have been present in the labor market for centuries. But as students explore their career outlook, they can examine new trends in the job market to determine what career would yield the most satisfaction in the future. Students might consider a specific career as they explore and enter college. However, as they delve more in their studies, they might change their mind especially if they want to pursue graduate studies or embrace a professional field such as medicine and law. As an illustration, a graduating high school senior wants to become a teacher and for that purpose, he majors in both

Mathematics and Computer Science. As he progresses in his studies, he explores career opportunities, future job outlook, and potential lifetime earnings. After his research, his focus shifts from the field of education to finance. He can use his background in Mathematics and Computer Science to work as a broker or a Wall Street trader.

Some majors offered in a community college setting enable students to immediately join the workforce upon completion. Examples include automotive, nursing, construction, paralegal studies and accounting. Holders of an Associate Degree in one of those fields can choose to pursue their education towards a Bachelor's degree or seek promotion opportunities within their jobs.

Holland Code	Sample 2-year College Majors	Sample 4-year College Majors
REALISTIC "The Doers" Who are they? People who have athletic or mechanical abilities prefer to work with objects, machines, tools, plants, or animals, or to be outdoors What do they like? Tinker with machines/vehicles Work outdoors Use their hands Be physically active Build things Tend/train animals Work on electronic equipment	Architectural Technology Automotive Service Specialist Computer Technology Computer Science Construction Technology Criminal Justice: Police Option Engineering & Technology: Fire Protection Technology Horticulture Landscape Development Manufacturing Physical Therapist Assistant	Aerospace Engineering Architectural Technology Aviation Civil Engineering Technology Computer Engineering Computer Network Administration Computer Science Computer Software Specialist Construction Engineering Technology Construction Science Dental Hygiene
INVESTIGATIVE "The Thinkers" Who are they? People who like to observe, learn, investigate, analyze, evaluate or solve problems What do they like to do? Explore a variety of ideas Use computers, Work independently Perform lab experiments Read scientific or technical journals Analyze data deal with abstractions Do research & be challenged	American Sign Language Health Information Technology Medical Assisting Nursing Occupational Therapy Assistant Veterinary Science Technology	Area Studies Anthropology Astronomy Astrophysics Biochemistry Bioengineering Biology Botany Chemical Engineering Chemistry Civil Engineering Computer Science & Engineering Criminology Dentistry Economics Electrical Engineering Environmental Sciences Foreign Languages Linguistics Nursing (all programs) Pharmacy Physics Pre-Medicine Pre-Dentistry Pre-Veterinary Medicine Psychology Sociology Veterinarian medicine Women's and Gender Studies Zoology

Holland Code	Sample 2-year College Majors	Sample 4-year College Majors
ARTISTIC	Communications and Media Arts	Architecture
"The Creators"	Fine Arts	Art
	Graphic Design	Art Education
	Interior Design	Art History
Who are they?	Photographic Imaging	Dance
People who have artistic,	Radio and Television Production	Drama
innovating or intuition	Technical Communication	English
abilities and like to work in	Performing Arts: Drama	English Education
unstructured situations using	Performing Arts: Music	Environmental Design
their imagination and creativity		Ethics and Religion
		Film/Video
		Foreign Language Education
What do they like to do?		Humanities
Attend concerts, theatres, and		Journalism and Mass Communication
art exhibits		Journalism: Broadcasting & Electronic
Read fiction, plays, and		Media
poetry, Work on crafts		Library-Media Education
Take photographs		Linguistics
Express themselves		Music
creatively.		Music Education
Deal with ambiguous ideas		Philosophy
		Religious Studies
		Theatre
SOCIAL	Community Service Assistant	Athletic Training
"The Helpers"	Community/Outdoor Recreation	Career & Technical Education
	Human Resources Mgmt.	Community Health
Who are they?	Recreation Leadership	Communication Disorders
People who like to work with	Travel & Tourism	Criminal Justice
people to enlighten, inform,		Emergency Medical Science Technology
help		Health and Exercise
		History
		Institutional Health Care
		Kinesiotherapy
		Nutrition
What do they like?		Physical Education
Work in groups,		Physical Therapy
Help people with problems		Public Administration
Participate in meetings		Science Education
Do volunteer work		Social Studies Education
Work with young people		Social Work
Play team sports		Speech Language Pathology
Serve others		Special Education
		Therapeutic Recreation

Holland Code	Sample 2-year College Majors	Sample 4-year College Majors
ENTERPRISING "The Decision Makers" Who are they? People who like to work with people, influencing, persuading, performing, leading or managing for organizational goals or economic gain What do they like? Make decisions affecting others Be elected to office Win a leadership or sales award Start their own service or business Campaign politically Meet important people Have power or status	Accounting Banking Sequence Business Administration Business Management Finance Insurance Management Marketing Office Management Real Estate Restaurant Management Retail Business Management	Business Administration Business Management Technology Electronic Commerce Entrepreneurship/Family & Small Business Finance Human Resource Management Industrial Engineering International Business Management Marketing Marketing & Sales Technology Operations Management Public Relations Pre-Law Public Affairs & Administration Public Affairs & Community Services Purchasing Urban Studies
CONVENTIONAL "The organizers" Who are they? People who like to work with data, have clerical or numerical ability, carry out tasks in detail, or follow through on others' instructions What do they like? Follow clearly defined procedures Use data processing equipment, Work with numbers Be responsible for details Collect or organize things	Computer Information Systems Food Service Administration Medical Records Paralegal Studies	Accounting Accounting Technology Administrative Office Technology Data Processing Economics Financial Services Information Systems Information Services and Support Legal Assisting/Pre-Law Studies Logistics & Management Management Information Systems Paralegal Studies Transportation Management Technology

Source: www.iseek.org and the University of Oklahoma Career Services

2. Skills

Students have to determine what they do well or competencies which they have an affinity or aptitude for. Innate or acquired through practice, talents can serve as guides for a major selection. For this purpose, they can be broken into three groups:

- People skills: serving, helping, speaking, negotiating, persuading, mentoring, supervising
- Data skills: computing, analyzing, synthetizing, forecasting
- Things skills: operating, fixing, setting up, handling, controlling

3. Values

Values are developed from an early age and are a reflection of what one holds as important in life. They are dynamic in the sense that they can be shaped and re-shaped by our experiences. Similar to skills, they can help a student figure out their college major and careers derived therefrom. The aim at this point is to know what is important to you, the student.

- Personal and family values: some majors lead to careers granting more time and flexibility to spend time with families.
- Cultural or religious values: for some people, religion plays an important role in their life. Therefore, it would be somehow improbable for a conservative Christian to thrive in a job advocating abortion or euthanasia (assisted-suicide).
- Economic values: if financial status is vital for a student, he or she should look into majors yielding some of the highest incomes on the pay scale. The US Bureau of Labor Statistics is a great resource in that regard.

4. Personality

It is the way you have been from birth. In terms of personality, two emerge. Either one is extrovert or introvert. Knowing their personality can help students narrow down their choices of college majors. Commonly, the results of the Myer Briggs Personality Test provide students an insight into who they are.

Sources of Energy	E	Extrovert	I	Introvert
		Attention is focused on the outer world of people and things		Attention is focused on the inner world of thoughts and reflections
Information Acquisition	S	Sensing	N	Intuition
		Information is processed through the five senses (sight, hearing, taste, smell, and touch)		Information is processed through a hunch or "sixth sense"
Decision Making	T	Thinking	F	Feeling
		Decisions are based on logic and impartial/objective analysis		Decisions are based on people and subjective in value
Orientation towards the Outer World	J	Judging	P	Perceiving
		Lifestyle is planned, organized, and decisive		Lifestyle is flexible, spontaneous, and adaptable

Source: Myers Briggs Personality Test

Takeaways from Chapter 6

- Graduating seniors don't need to have a definite major prior to completing their college application.
- However, they should know some colleges have very competitive programs or high impacted majors where admission is very selective with some students on the waiting list.
- It is not uncommon for professionals to change careers many times in their lifetime, and across different major fields of study.
- College students can major simultaneously in two fields of study. To graduate in a timely manner, they should disclose that plan from their freshman year to their advisor so that their educational plan reflects that goal.
- The four common ways that students can explore college majors are interests, skills, values, and personality.

The RIASEC TEST Student Worksheet – Chapter 6

Read each statement. If you agree with the statement, circle the appropriate box. There are no wrong answers! Record your scores in the appropriate box at the bottom of the table to know some of your career pathways.

	1	2	3	4	5	6
A	I like to work on cars.	I like to do puzzles.	I am good at working independently.	I like to work in teams.	I am an ambitious person.	I like to organize things (files, desks).
B	I like to build things.	I like to do experiments.	I like to draw.	I like to teach or train people.	I like to try to influence or persuade other people.	I like to have clear instructions to follow.
C	I like to take care of animals.	I enjoy science.	I enjoy creative writing.	I like trying to help people solve their problems.	I like selling things.	I wouldn't mind working 8 hours per day in an office.
D	I like putting things together or assemble things.	I enjoy trying to figure out how things work.	I like to read about art and music.	I am interested in healing people.	I am quick to take on new responsibilities.	I pay attention to details.
E	I like to cook.	I like to analyze things (problems/situations).	I like to play instruments or sing.	I enjoy learning about other cultures.	I would like to start my own business.	I like to do filing or typing.
F	I am a practical person.	I like working with numbers or charts.	I like acting in plays.	I like to get into discussions about issues.	I like to lead.	I am good at keeping records of my work.
G	I like working outdoors.	I'm good at math.	I am a creative person.	I like helping people.	I like to give speeches.	I would like to work in an office.
	R	I	A	S	E	C
							←Total

My Highest 3 Codes are: _____   _____   _____

Source: Hawaii Public Schools and Ohio Adult Basic and Literacy Education (ABLE) Program

Chapter 7

Paying for College

Applying to college is complex but paying for higher education is even more difficult for immigrants in the United States. College costs remain a critical factor in college attendance. As students commit to specific schools where they want to undertake their studies, parents must ensure that there is enough money to cover their expenses for a minimum of four years. The common ways college education can be financed are 529 plans, financial aid, state aid, and scholarships.

A. 529 Savings Plan

Parents are encouraged to save for their child college tuition. The plan known as the 529 plan is a savings program operated by states and specific educational institutions to help families afford the high cost of a college education. Not all colleges and universities participate in this program; thus, parents must research schools that embrace this initiative. A simple way is to first lookup the college federal code from the Federal Student Aid website. From there it becomes easier to find out if the institution is eligible for a 529 plan. These saving plans are applicable not only to schools located on continental US but equally to some schools overseas. Having a 529 plan that extends overseas can further help a student who would like to study abroad in college. 529 plans might vary from state to state. Family members desiring to start one for their child should select the option suitable to their family circumstances. Spatial mobility is common in the United States and a family can start a 529 savings plan within a specific state and later establish residency to a new one. It would be wise for subscribers to understand the terms of the plan should such circumstance arises in the future, or should the beneficiary i.e. child or grandchild decides to attend college out-of-state. Given that 529 plans are incentives with tax advantages, parents are strongly encouraged to consult with their tax advisor for more information on their process. It is never too early to start a college savings plan. On its website, the Internal Revenue Service (IRS) provides detailed information on who can set up the account, be a beneficiary, and what the contribution limits can be.

School Year	State	Schools
2016-2017	Maryland	Frostburg University
	Maryland	Goucher College
	Maryland	Morgan State University
	Washington DC	Catholic University of America
	Washington DC	Gallaudet University
	Washington DC	University of the District of Columbia
	Virginia	Hollins University
	Virginia	Longwood University
	Virginia	Randolph-Macon College

Table 35: Sample schools accepting 529 Plans (School Year 2016-2017)

B. Federal Aid

The Federal Government provides assistance via the Free Application for Federal Student Aid (FAFSA). There is no cost associated with this form. To begin with, students must have genuine social security numbers to apply for the program. More, they must be either US citizens or permanent residents. Students with specific residency statuses should check with either the Counselor or the College and Career staff at school to know more about their eligibility. Funds received via the financial aid process are not free money to pursue a college education. The financial aid package consists of various types of aid: Pell grants, loans, and work-study. Pell grant money doesn't have to be reimbursed.

Students and/or parents can contract loans. They come in two categories: subsidized and unsubsidized. In the first type, no interest is accrued while the student is in school. In the second, the interest accrued must be paid while the student is in school. Depending upon the terms of the agreement, loans must be repaid sometime after the student's college graduation. Work-study provides students with the opportunity to apply for campus-based job positions depending upon their availability. Positions are not guaranteed but that advantage can help a student meet some of his or her basic needs. In some instances, a FAFSA applicant might only be eligible for a Direct Plus Loan. The terms and conditions of this parent loan might vary from college to college. Parents are expected to contact the financial aid office to know their requirements. Direct Plus Loans might involve a credit history check. People with adverse credit history including but not limited to bankruptcy, foreclosure, and wages garnishment can be eligible for the loan. An endorser might be required as part of the application process. Additional documentation might be needed on an individual basis as well.

The window to complete the FAFSA opens up on October 1 for graduating seniors. Prior to get started with the application, parents and students are encouraged to get an FSA ID that would serve as their electronic signature. It is a personal identifier linked to their social security number and should not be shared with anyone. Using someone else's FSA ID is a fraudulent act in the eyes of the federal government. Second, they should collect all documents relevant for the FAFSA application per se. Examples include:

- Driver's License (if applicable)
- Permanent Resident Card (if applicable)
- Previous year tax income
- W-2 forms or other records of money earned (if available)
- Untaxed income records (Social Security Administration, Temporary Assistance for Needy Families/TANF, Welfare, Veterans Benefits Records (if applicable)
- Previous year bank statements (if applicable)
- Previous year mortgage information, business, farms, stocks, bonds, investment records (if applicable)

Once all documents are compiled, both student and parent must complete the FAFSA because there are sections specifically reserved for each party. At the end of the process, both would electronically sign the form (using their FSA IDs) and submit it for review by the US Department of Education. Upon submission, they would know what the Expected Family Contribution (EFC) for the family is. Based on tax and other information provided on the FAFSA, it is the minimum amount of money the federal government believes the family can contribute towards their child's education that academic year. Families with very low income might have an EFC of zero (0), which means the family has the greater need to help pay for their child's college education. Within a short timeframe, the student should receive via email the Student Aid Report (SAR), which acknowledges the reception of the FAFSA application. If there are pieces of information missing, he or she should act promptly by taking the necessary steps.

For illustration, let's take the case of Joy a high school senior graduating in June 2017. After the FAFSA window opened for the 2017-2018 school year, Joy submitted her application using her parents 2015 tax information in October 2016. By using the IRS data retrieval tool, tax information from the IRS would automatically transfer into her FAFSA. This process is very delicate; therefore, parents and students alike are encouraged to attend free workshops to become educated by professionals in the field about the process. Moreover, they can secure free assistance with completing the FAFSA.

In the past, the timeline allowed students to complete all their college applications by winter break and get started on the FAFSA process in January. As the timeline has shifted to October of the senior year, students should research their colleges of interest no later than the summer prior to their senior year so that all prospective colleges are listed on their FAFSA applications in the initial submission. Students should be familiar with all financial aid priority deadlines: federal, state, and schools. The sooner the FAFSA is completed, the higher the chances of receiving the maximum aid for which one is eligible. Students should update the FAFSA every time they make a change. It can be as simplistic as removing or adding a new college to their list or correcting parental financial information. Financial Counseling is required prior to the disbursement of financial aid monies to students and before they graduate from college. Students and parents should borrow responsibly, and students can decline to take loans. If a student decides not to accept the loans awarded on the financial aid package, he or she must inform the financial aid office of the decision as soon possible so that the funds can be re-allocated to other students in need.

C. State Aid

Jurisdictions in the DMV provide tuition assistance grants to graduating seniors. Need or non-need based, the amounts of these grants vary from year to year depending upon the available funding and so does the list of approved institutions. Students must meet all the eligibility criteria and submit all required documentation by the deadline. Parents must be familiar with the conditions attached to the award. For instance, in the state of Maryland, students have a specific time to accept or decline MD-CAPS awards.

State	Program	Managing Agency
MD	Maryland College Aid Processing System (MD-CAPS)	Maryland Higher Education Commission
DC	DC Tuition Assistance Grant (DC TAG)	Office of the State Superintendent of Education
VA	Virginia Tuition Assistance Grant (VTAG)	State Council of Higher Education in Virginia

Table 36: DC Area state tuition assistance administrators

D. Scholarships

Scholarships represent an additional means to secure money for college. Scholarship search is an arduous task that thankfully yields high benefits. The results would be even greater should students and parents collaboratively work throughout this process. Within schools, the staff at the College and Career Center is one of the gateways to scholarship opportunities. They send regular emails to students and parents informing them of scholarship opportunities. All parents/guardians of seniors should ensure that they are included on the mailing list at their child's school so as not to miss scholarship announcements. Multiple scholarship search engines exist online. Students must inquire about their genuine nature before signing up. The staff at the College and Career center can help spot scammers that are only after money and private information. Both students and parents must understand that a sizable portion of scholarship are merit-based. This underscores the strength of an academic record and standardized test scores. The more complete a scholarship profile is, the more scholarship matches a student receives. Many community organizations, corporations, department stores, property management corporations, utility companies, banks, grocery store chains, religious groups, professional organizations, sororities and fraternities offer scholarships to students within their community. Local scholarship opportunities remain the best to compete for as the number of applicants is lower compared to those competing for national scholarships.

Elected representatives constitute another source for scholarships. Students should contact local elected officials for scholarship opportunities. State representatives in the State of Maryland i.e. Senators and Delegates offer scholarship opportunities to graduating seniors. However, the student must directly contact the senator and delegate of his or her district of residence to receive the application. Essays are frequently required and it is crucial for students beginning 9th grade to hone their writing skills because they can help secure monies to help pay for college in the future. Moreover, they should attend scholarship conferences or workshops within their community. Undocumented students can secure scholarships to help pay for college thanks to organizations that raise funds for that specific purpose within the community.

E. College Scholarship Service Profile (CSS Profile)

Beside the federal government, other entities provide scholarships and loan options to cover college expenses. To access this information, students would have to create a profile with College Board. Some schools, particularly in cases of early decision and early action, require a CSS profile for an accurate assessment of the financial needs of the student. Unlike the FAFSA that is free, the CSS profile application initially costs $25 to send to one college or scholarship program. For additional reports, the student would have to pay $16 for each.

State	Schools	CCS Profile priority deadline
Maryland	Johns Hopkins University	November 15 (Early Decision) February 1 (Regular Decision)
Washington DC	Catholic University of America	December 1 (Early Decision) December 1 (Early Action) February 1 (Regular Decision)
Virginia	College of Williams and Mary	November 15 (Early Decision) February 1 (Regular Decision)

Table 37: Sample CSS Profile deadlines (School Year 2016-2017)

F. Elements of a Financial Aid Package

In the spring, seniors who have completed their FAFSA in a timely manner start to receive their financial aid award letters. These letters provide details on the cost of attendance (tuition, fees, room and board, books, supplies, transportation, and other expenses,) grants, loans, work-study, and scholarships awarded to the student. Schools would try to meet the need of the student as much as they can. However, in case of a balance, the parents are responsible to come up with the money.

Scenario 1: Award letter without scholarships

The following sample financial letter represents an award package where the student earned no scholarships to offset the cost of the post-secondary education. The total cost of attendance is estimated at $32,932. The total amount of awards is lower at $24,800. The gap of $8132 between the estimated awards and the cost of attendance is the responsibility of parents. If they can afford it, the student might go to that school otherwise, both student and parents would have to revisit their college choice to a more affordable school.

	Fall 2017	Spring 2018	Total
Tuition and Fees	$8,756	$8,756	$17,512
Room and Board	$5,435	$5,435	$10,870
Books and Supplies	$725	$725	$1,450
Personal Expenses	$800	$800	$1,600
Transportation	$750	$750	$1,500
Total Cost of Attendance			**$32,932**
Federal Pell Grant	$2,500	$2,500	$5,000
Federal Work Study	$1,000	$1,000	$2,000
Subsidized Loan	$2,000	$2,000	$4,000
Unsubsidized Loan	$900	$900	$1,800
Parent Loan	$6,000	$6,000	$12,000
Estimated Total Awards			**$24,800**

Table 38: Sample financial aid award letter without scholarships

Scenario 2: Award letter with multiple scholarships

In this example, the student earned various scholarships from modest to considerable amounts. The cost of attendance is $32,932 but the estimated number of awards boosted by scholarships earnings amounts to $44,400. With $11,468 available, student and parents have more leverage in college affordability.

	Fall 2017	Spring 2018	Total
Tuition and Fees	$8,756	$8,756	$17,512
Room and Board	$5,435	$5,435	$10,870
Books and Supplies	$725	$725	$1,450
Personal Expenses	$800	$800	$1,600
Transportation	$750	$750	$1,500
Total Cost of Attendance			**$32,932**

Honors Scholarship	$7,000	$7,000	$14,000
XYZ Scholarship	$1,200	$1,200	$2,400
ABC Scholarship	$300	$300	$600
Grocery Store Scholarship	$200	$200	$400
Greek Life Scholarship	$500	$500	$1,000
Gas Company Scholarship	$200	$200	$400
Church Scholarship	$400	$400	$800
Federal Pell Grant	$2,500	$2,500	$5,000
Federal Work Study	$1,000	$1,000	$2,000
Subsidized Loan	$2,000	$2,000	$4,000
Unsubsidized Loan	$900	$900	$1,800
Parent Plus Loan	$6,000	$6,000	$12,000
Estimated Total Awards			**$44,400**

Table 39: Sample financial aid award letter including scholarships

• Do I need to complete the FAFSA?

Some families estimate their incomes to be so high that they view completing FAFSA as a waste of time. Educators encourage all students regardless of their family financial background to complete the FAFSA. Many colleges refer to the FAFSA to disburse some of the institutional aid to deserving students. If parents have filed their taxes, the student should be proactive and have a FAFSA on record.

G. Hidden Costs of College

So far, this guide has shared some of the college application costs at the high school level. Test prep, SAT or ACT test registration, AP exams, college applications, request for test scores to be sent to colleges, transcripts, CCS profile are some of the ones covered earlier. As parents develop their budget for a college education for their child, other items that should be included in the forecast most of times are missing. Including these items in the college budget help in creating a more accurate budget for the college-bound senior.

1. Health insurance

College students must have health insurance especially those residing on campus. Students might be prevented from registering for classes if that requirement is not met. Consequently, if a student is not covered by his or her parents' insurance, the family must work together to get the student insured. Some insurance providers specifically tailor health plans for college students. In searching for the best quote, parents should examine the network of hospitals and physicians in the plan and determine if it includes prescription and preventive care.

2. Transportation

The cost of attendance estimates transportation fees for a student during an academic year. Students who have a car they want to take on campus must inquire about the parking policy of their universities, as some might not provide parking privileges to freshmen. Parking privileges might involve a fee, which must be included in the monthly budget for the student. More, a car means gas, insurance and maintenance, which parents must budget should their child be away in college. During holidays, students travel back home by car, train, or plane, all of which involve some expenses. During winter, spring, or summer break, some students like to travel around and parents might have to pay for their child's transportation needs. On campus, car rental or car sharing options incur fees that might be paid by parents' allowances.

3. Electronics

All college students want to have personal computers loaded with the recent software enabling them to succeed academically. The rapid pace with which technology changes makes many electronic devices obsolete within a short time. Smartphones, tablets, kindle, remain additional tools parents might have to maintain and update on a regular basis for the comfort of the college student.

4. Appliances

Living arrangements in college particularly for freshmen are straightforward. Regardless of their room plan, they want to enjoy some of the benefits of modern life. If the school doesn't provide some appliances for comfort living, students would likely turn to parents for their purchase. Small fridge, microwave, juice blender, coffee maker, and irons remain prized by students.

5. Furniture

Once again, dorm rooms vary from one college to another and within colleges depending upon grade level and room plan. Some students might want to purchase lamps, nighstands, and bedding. That adds up to a long list of items not spelled out on the cost of attendance.

6. Clothing

For some college students, parents support changes in wardrobe although they might live miles away from one another.

7. Food and beverages

Besides their board plans, college students in general love to socialize around meals, parties, and other festivities. These gatherings involve the consumption of foodstuffs and drinks that parents might indirectly purchase.

8. Entertainment

Occasionally, academics take a back seat for college students who carve out some precious time to relax. Regardless of the form of entertainment they favor, some students get money from their parents to enjoy the dolce vita.

Takeaways from Chapter 7

- 529 savings plan, grants, loans, and scholarships help pay for a college education in the United States.
- The FAFSA is a free application while the CSS profile requires an application fee and additional fees to send to schools or scholarship programs of interest.
- Some schools require the CSS profile and the FAFSA. Both aid forms might have different deadlines.
- The FSA ID is a personal electronic signature for the FAFSA and should never be shared with anyone.
- FAFSA applications are now available on October 1.
- The student must complete the FAFSA every year while in college.
- All jurisdictions in the DMV offer grant opportunities to eligible graduating seniors: MD-CAPS in Maryland, DC TAG in Washington DC and VTAG in Virginia.
- Grants funds don't have to be reimbursed, but students must maintain satisfactory academic progress for their renewal.
- Scholarship opportunities are available in various platforms in the community but students must be diligent in completing each one for which they are eligible.
- Parents are responsible for covering the difference between the cost of attendance and the expected family contribution.
- Students can decline loans so long as they inform the financial aid office of their decision as soon as possible.
- College attendance has additional costs that remain under the radar until students are about to move in their dorm.

Parent and Student Worksheet # 1 – Chapter 7

Complete together to create a timeline to complete your financial aid forms.

	School	State	FAFSA Priority Deadline	CSS Priority Deadline (if applicable)	State Aid Priority Deadline
1					
2					
3					
4					
5					
6					
7					
8					
9					
10					
11					
12					
13					
14					
15					

Parent and Student Worksheet # 2 – Chapter 7

Elements of a Financial Aid Package

Using the financial aid estimator of all colleges you are considering complete the following table as much as you can. Bear in mind that not all information will be immediately available to you.

College	COA (Cost of Attendance)	EFC (Expected Family Contribution)	Financial Aid Package					Total Awards	Gap between COA and EFC = Parents Contribution
			Pell Grant	Subsidized Loan	Unsubsidized Loan	Scholarships	Work Study		

Parent and Student Worksheet # 3 – Chapter 7

Compare College Costs to determine your best financially fit school.

Name of College	College 1	College 2	College 3	College 4	College 5
Tuition					
Fees					
Room (Dorm)					
Board (Meal Plan)					
Books & Supplies					
Health Insurance					
Appliances					
Cellphone Service					
Computer/Laptop					
Bedding					
Clothing					
Groceries					
Transportation					
Personal expenses					
Entertainment					
Total Annual Cost of Attendance					

Rate your 3 best financially fit schools

1: _____ 2: _____ 3: _____

Chapter 8

American High School Experience

So long as a parent is familiar with their child's school's calendar, some events occur annually. But what do they mean?

A. Traditions

1. Homecoming

Usually occurring in the fall, it celebrates alumni (former graduates) and current students in a school. It involves numerous cultural and sports events, particularly American football. There might also be a homecoming dance during which both a homecoming queen and homecoming king are chosen.

2. Spirit week

It is a week during which schools organize various activities to promote school pride. Students can dress up along various themes (professional day, jersey day, twin day, pajama day, superhero day, and historic figure day) or with class colors. In most high schools, the event includes a pep rally in the gymnasium.

3. Senior Class Trip

To celebrate the completion of high school, seniors might travel to a destination chosen based on school's guidelines. The trip can be overnight with school staff, administrators, and volunteer parents all acting as chaperones. However, parents should be aware of the financial contribution required from their child to cover their portion of the trip as well as the payment deadline.

4. Field Day

It offers an opportunity for students to engage in team-building exercises outside of the classroom. Generally, students enjoy the day visiting various stations and engaging in collective sports and outdoors activities.

5. Prom

It is a formal and the most important dance of the senior year. It can be quite expensive. Some of the common costs are the prom cover charge, a limousine rental, flowers, corsage, formal gown, professional make-up, and hairdressing for ladies, tuxedo and other black tie attire for gentlemen. Prom night might include an after-prom party. For some, it is an official rite of passage from adolescence into adulthood.

6. Driver's License

On average, the minimum driving age in US States is 16 years old. In other words, students in 10th grade can drive alone to and from school if they have met their state requirements.

7. Fundraising

It is not uncommon for students to engage in various activities to raise money to finance some of their activities. The most common are bake/cookies/chocolate/donuts/coffee/lemonade/pizza sale.

8. Fees

Parents should expect their children to be cleared for all financial obligations prior to their graduation. The process includes paying for the graduation fees, cap and gown, yearbook (if interested), fines and other dues owed to the school.

B. Pitfalls

Students face some hazards in American high schools of which parents should be aware.

1. Social promotion

In some cases, grades might not be an accurate assessment of a student's knowledge. For a myriad of reasons, one of them being the reluctance to fail students, some teachers assign passing grades to undeserving students. It is up to parents to ensure that their children earn an education instead of being passed on to the next grade without acquiring proper knowledge and skill mastery.

2. Bullying

Sadly, physical, verbal, emotional, and cyber bullying are regular occurrences in high school. There is a zero tolerance for bullying, and if parents suspect instances of bullying or even better, if their children open up and express that they are being bullied by peers, or know of a student being bullied at school, the parent must contact the school counselor and administrator immediately for follow-up. Speaking up is essential to stop further victims and fatalities.

3. Gangs

Gang membership with varying degrees of visibility can be an issue in some high schools where it can breed violence. Schools usually organize campaigns and workshops to sensitize students and the community against the dangers associated with gang life.

4. Drugs

It is not uncommon for teenagers to be in possession of legal and illegal drugs. Students can lay their hands on these substances via a doctor's prescription, by attending parties where they are available, or simply through peers or dealers. Campaigns against drug use are common in schools and the larger community. However, if there is any suspicion of drug use, parents should seek help immediately with the medical staff. School counselors and social workers could be one of the sources for extra help.

5. Underage drinking

In the United States, the drinking age depends on the state law. However, some high schoolers successfully purchase alcohol by using a myriad of tricks. Its unchecked consumption can lead to accidents, dependency, and even fatalities.

6. Teen pregnancy

Attitudes towards sex in American society may be viewed by some African parents as very liberal in comparison to their country of origin. They should be aware that in some schools, to simultaneously prevent teen pregnancies and sexually transmitted diseases, condoms might be distributed without restrictions by the school nurse. In other words, a student can request on their own volition free condoms to protect themselves against unintended consequences from sex. Again, the policy is not streamlined and parents should familiarize themselves with strategies in place at their child's school.

7. Digital footprint

Nowadays, students can connect to a wide array of online networks primarily for social purposes. In addition to various online predators hovering over unsuspecting adolescents, it is important to mention that online activities can become obstacles to realizing one's fullest potential. Increasingly, colleges and scholarship organizations scour the Internet in search of compromising information on applicants. Words, pictures, and other online materials deemed offensive or not up to appropriate standards of conduct can deny a student entrance to the college of their dream or access to a scholarship that can alleviate the high cost of college.

C. Non-Academic resources

High schools in the DMV area offer a wide selection of resources for students and parents to get acclimated to the American way of life. Their breadth covers physical, emotional, and mental health. In addition to the nurse on campus, some schools offer free day care for students-parents. Social workers assist with numerous issues such as depression, suicide ideation, abuse, violence, and other non-academic issues that might affect a student's academic success. Mental health personnel are available for those who might need that service. Schools can also direct parents and students to community organizations or governmental agencies that provide free English Language classes for adults, housing assistance, food bank, and donation centers for some parents that might experience difficult times. Again, language should not be a barrier. The DMV area is one of the most linguistically and culturally diverse of the United States. Therefore, schools have put in place strategies to provide the best customer service possible to all parents regardless of their primary language.

Student Only Worksheet – Chapter 8

Please answer the following questions to assess your involvement in your school traditions.

Key Points	Responses
What special activities do you participate in during homecoming or spirit week at school and that can be used in your college application?	
What fundraising activities are you involved in and that demonstrate school community involvement?	
What steps do you take to remain safe online?	
What are some elements of your school's bullying policy?	
Are there obvious signs of gang activity at your school? How do you know?	
According to your school, what should you do if one of your friends or classmates talks about suicide?	
Does your school organize a senior class trip?	☐ Yes ☐ No ☐ I don't know
Seniors only: If you answered yes to the previous question, what is the destination for the current year?	
Seniors only: What would be the cover charge of your prom?	
Seniors only: What is the deadline to pay for your senior fees?	

Parent Only Worksheet – Chapter 8

Key Points	Responses
What reservations or concerns if any do you have on some of the traditions in American high schools?	_____ _____ _____ _____
Are you familiar with your child's Internet activities?	☐ Yes ☐ No ☐ Somewhat
If you are, how do you ensure that your child maintains a proper digital footprint?	_____ _____
If you are not, how do you make sure that online presence doesn't compromise your child's future?	_____ _____
Select all topics you have discussed with your child.	☐ Bullying ☐ Drug consumption ☐ Gang activity ☐ Internet safety ☐ Underage drinking ☐ Teen pregnancy
Select all activities your child has been involved in:	☐ Bullying ☐ Drug consumption ☐ Drug trafficking ☐ Gang activity ☐ Underage drinking ☐ Neither
To the best of your knowledge are condoms available to your child at school?	☐ Yes ☐ No ☐ I don't know
Of all temptations faced by teenagers, which one worries you the most and why?	_____ _____ _____
Would you be comfortable speaking with a mental health professional should behavior concerns arise about your child? Why or why not?	_____ _____
If it were possible to secure a car, how comfortable are you having your child drive to and from school? Explain your answer.	_____ _____ _____

Chapter 9

Parental Involvement

Parents are full partners in their child's education. Ideally, they are expected to participate and communicate as much as possible with school staff about their child's academic progress. Regardless of their busy schedule, it is up to parents to keep up with occurrences at the school. Language should not be a deterrent for a lack of follow-up because school districts in the DMV area provide translators free of charge to parents for all interactions with school personnel. Parental participation can take two forms: visibility and communication.

A. Visibility at School

When a child begins high school, it is crucial for parents to attend the new student orientation. Information shared in that venue will facilitate their understanding of the school's culture, structure, and more, of the expectations set for each pupil. Every academic year, there is a *back to school night* during which parents meet their children's support system (teachers, counselors, and administrators). The event is structured and parents get the opportunity to visit their child's classrooms and become acquainted with all the school-based resources available for academic success. Grade-level parent meetings supplement the information provided during the meeting. Specifically, the school administration provides parents with requirements and expectations pertaining to 9th graders, 10th graders, 11th graders or 12th graders. Depending upon the school, back to school night might include grade level introductory meetings. In other words, during the back to school night, part of the evening could be devoted to grade level meetings so that parents make the acquaintance of administrators, counselors, and teachers supporting their child during that academic year. Parents of juniors and seniors are strongly encouraged to attend financial aid workshops to explore available opportunities to finance their child's college education. As a reminder, those workshops can touch on various types of scholarships opportunities available to students. Last but not the least, parent associations represent another forum through which relatives can volunteer in many capacities including translation services, hospitality, and chaperones for various events such as field trips, sports tournaments, dances, plays, and prom.

B. Communication with the School

Undoubtedly, like their American counterparts, African parents are busy securing a decent living for their offspring. However, that should never be used as an excuse not to keep up with a child's academic progress. Regular check-ins with the school staff can take various forms.

- o Teacher: schedule a meeting with teachers to discuss the student's academic progress and challenges. Some schools might provide this opportunity during Parent-Teacher Conferences.
- o Counselor: schedule a meeting with the counselor to discuss your child's goals, class changes, or college application process. This is particularly important for juniors transitioning into their last year of high school so that students can successfully follow a timeline to graduation.
- o College and Career Coordinator: schedule a meeting to discuss college aid financial options, scholarship opportunities, college visits and college tours.
- o Email: a parent can elect to receive notices from teachers, counselors and the college and career coordinator via email. However, they need to check their inbox on a regular basis and acknowledge the reception of important emails requiring prompt action.
- o Phone: update your information with the school in case of emergency.

o   Electronic grade book: many schools provide parents with the opportunity to check their child's grades online. Protocols vary from one school to another but this method is another opportunity to stay involved in their child's academic experience. As such, parents can have crucial conversations before the student's grades take a deep dive.

o   Website: schools update salient information on their website. Parents are encouraged to check out this source of information they can access at their own convenience.

By Stéphanie Mbella

Parental Involvement Assessment Chapter 9

Please respond to the following questions to assess your involvement with your child's high school.

Key Points	Options	
Did you attend back to school night this academic year?	☐ Yes	☐ No
Did you attend the grade level meeting this academic year?	☐ Yes	☐ No
Are you a member of the school's PTA or PTSA?	☐ Yes	☐ No
If yes, when was the last PTA or PTSA meeting you attended this academic year?	_____	
Are you on the parents' listserv?	☐ Yes	☐ No
Do you participate in other school's activities?	☐ Yes	☐ No
Have you volunteered at your child's high school this academic year?	☐ Yes	☐ No
Do you have online access to your child's grades?	☐ Yes	☐ No
How often do you check your child's grades online?	☐ Regularly ☐ Occasionally ☐ Never	
Are you comfortable talking to teachers about your child?	☐ Yes	☐ No
When was the last conference you had with your child's teacher?	_____	
How often do you email your child's teachers?	☐ Regularly ☐ Occasionally ☐ Never	
Have you met with your child's Counselor this year?	☐ Yes	☐ No
When was the last conference you had with your child's teachers?	_____	
How often do you visit your child's high school website?	☐ Regularly ☐ Occasionally ☐ Never	

Chapter 10

College Readiness and Career Readiness

Students in American high schools are extremely busy. Between academics, sports, clubs, community service, jobs, hobbies, and family obligations, some high schoolers struggle to maintain a healthy balance. It does not come as a surprise when at the end of their secondary school coursework, students and parents need to determine if the student is college ready.

College readiness refers to the academic skill set all high school graduates should have mastered for a successful transition into post-secondary institutions. College ready students are expected to score at the college level in standardized testing (ACT, SAT or AP exams) or in placements tests such as the Accuplacer. Success hinges amongst other upon the depth and breadth of their skills in reading, writing, mathematics, science, and social studies. A student without college ready scores may be required to take remedial courses, which cost money and time. For illustration purposes, let's examine the case of two high school graduates Daniel and Chris whose 4 year-college requires a placement test for all incoming freshmen regardless of their scores on standardized testing. Chris scored below college on the placement exam while Daniel scored at the college level.

Students	Level	First semester	Second semester	Expected college graduation time
Daniel	College level	College classes	College classes	4 years
Chris	Below college-level	Remedial courses	Remedial courses	5 years

Table 40: Negative impacts of remedial courses

157

Daniel, who is college ready, is likely to graduate on time. However, Chris would spend one year working and paying for remedial courses thereby delaying his graduation timeline. Students with numerous remedial courses might get discouraged and interrupt their studies. Some end up at time with student loans that they would have to reimburse without a degree the loans were expected to help pay for. In addition to the content knowledge, college ready students must demonstrate employability skills that would help them be marketable in the labor force. Some of the competencies thought to be solely for the workplace in some cases drive academic success. The suggestions herein provided can be applied for the college environment and even beyond.

- Learning Style

As they prepare to transition in the workforce and university world, students should be aware of their learning styles. Humans are endowed with all learning styles however one or two might be the most dominant in an individual.
   o Visual learner: person who learns best when he or she can see the information presented in such forms as images, diagrams, charts, or other forms of graphics.
   o Auditory learner: person who learns best when he or she hears the information presented.
   o Kinesthetic learner: person who learns best when he or she uses the hands to manipulate objects, touch and feel the material, or move during activities.

Both college readiness and career readiness encompass the skill set college-bound students should possess as they leave high school. Though their focus is different, they have more converging than diverging points.

College Readiness Skills	Common Skills	Career Readiness Skills
Reading	Goal setting	Resume
Writing	Organization	Cover letter
Mathematics	Time management	Customer service
Science	Computer	Job search
Social Studies	Communication	Interview
Colleges ready scores in tests (ACT,	Planning	Reference request
SAT, AP, Accuplacer)	Problem-solving	
Study	Public speaking	
Test-taking	Teamwork	
Note-taking	Professionalism	
	Critical thinking	
	Self-awareness	
	Self-advocacy	

Table 41: Comparison between college readiness and career readiness skill sets

Both college readiness and career readiness require that students develop habits for success.

• Goal Setting

The primary goal of a high school student is to graduate in a timely manner. Every school year, he or she must successfully pass all classes to reach that objective. Students usually have multiple goals throughout an academic year, but they must know what resources they need to get started and devise a plan to achieve their objectives efficiently. Every student is unique and so is his or her academic path. However, there are some key actions per grade to prepare and ensure the smoothest transition possible from high school to college.

Grade	Semester 1	Semester 2
9 (Freshman)	Maintain good grades Sign up for after school tutoring or Saturday School for help Meet with guidance counselor Explore options for challenging courses	Maintain good grades Explore membership opportunities in clubs Start preparing for the PSAT College visits if possible
10 (Sophomore)	Maintain good grades Sign up for after school tutoring or Saturday School for help Meet with counselor Enroll in challenging courses (AP and Honors Courses) Register and take the PSAT Volunteer/community service Membership in clubs at school	Maintain good grades Prepare and Register for AP exams Attend College Fairs and visits Volunteer/community service Membership in clubs at school
11 (Junior)	Maintain good grades Sign up for after school tutoring or Saturday School for help Meet with counselor Register and take the PSAT Explore colleges of interest Complete a career interest survey Attend college fairs on and off campus Visit prospective colleges if possible Attend college open houses Volunteer/community service Membership in clubs at school	Maintain good grades Begin a prep class: SAT or ACT Take the SAT or ACT Create a professional resume Attend college fairs, open houses, college visits Talk to teachers about future college recommendation letters Develop an initial college list Look at admissions requirements in schools of interest Review admissions requirements and application deadlines of schools on college list Draft college application essays in the summer for early decision/early action Complete a summer internship Volunteer/community service Membership in clubs at schools
12 (Senior)	Maintain good grades Sign up for after school tutoring or Saturday School for help Meet with counselor to ensure all graduation requirements are met. Review admissions requirements in schools of interest Complete all college applications Take the SAT or ACT Complete the FAFSA Complete CSS Profile (if applicable) Complete scholarship applications Membership in clubs at schools	Maintain good grades Complete state aid application Complete scholarship applications College Placement Exam Preparation (Accuplacer and TOEFL) Review college acceptance letters Review college financial aid award offers Review state aid award offers Review scholarship awards letters Commit to a college by May 1st and send out deposit Send out housing deposit Request final high school transcript to be sent to the college selected for fall

Table 42: Sample action items per grade for college-bound students

- Organization Skills

Being organized is one of the key for success in life. Each individual sorts out things differently. However, each high school student, regardless of his or her living accommodations should create and maintain an environment conducive to academic success.

o Home: each student should have a specific place where he or she keeps the school materials. More, the student should dispose of a clutter-free space in the residence where he or she can do homework.

o Locker: students are assigned lockers for their personal use. They are subjected to the school's policies. For efficiency purposes, students should keep them clutter-free meaning lockers should not be clogged by clothing, shoes, food, beverages, candy wrappers, and other miscellaneous items.

o Backpack: it is important not to dump haphazardly stacks of sheets or loose-leaf papers in the bag. They might become difficult to sort out and frustration can lead the student to get rid of important information. Moreover, refrain from carrying beverages to avoid spills that can destroy documents.

o Class notes: students should either have a specific notebook per class or if using a binder for all classes, use divider tabs preferably with pockets to keep notes from each class separate.

o Handouts: often, teachers distribute handouts as supplementary materials for a lesson. For each handout received, students should record the date of reception, three-hole punched the document and insert it in the appropriate tab in the binder.

o Homework folder: a specific folder containing all homework helps in tracking down the completion of all assignments due.

o Drive (USB, computer, online drive): for every school year, students who maintain their work virtually should have a folder for every academic year i.e. freshman, sophomore, junior, and senior years. Within each year, students should create folders for each course. Those who are even more detail-oriented can divide their class folders into sections for quarters or notes, homework, papers, scholarships, or college essays.

- Time Management Skills

Time management is critical to reduce stress, avoid cramming in the last minute and to become effective in one's endeavors. General tips for successful time management for high school students include:

o Daily planner: to record all appointments, assignments and their due dates, test, quizzes, and exam dates, holidays, and other special events (practice, games, club meetings, work schedule). Students should cross out all completed assignments, tasks, or past activities to avoid confusion. For a better use, information must be updated accordingly, preferably on a weekly basis.

o Electronic calendar: some students are comfortable recording due dates on cellphones, email account, or other electronic devices. The student should set reminders early enough to complete the task.

- Note-taking skills

It is not uncommon for high school students to receive handouts in lieu of writing down their own notes in class. Students should be reminded that in college, each student is responsible for recording his or her personal notes. Instructors seldom share their lecture notes or provide handouts to supplement their lessons. Therefore, in preparation for college, students should try some of the following:

o Develop a personal note-taking system because that is the expectation in college.

o   Interact with the reading materials: as you are reading, get into the habit of underlying important passages, writing on the margins of the text, recording questions, highlighting new vocabulary words to include in a personal glossary.

o   Cornell Notes: students who lack effective note-taking skills should consider the Cornell method, which is very simple. In this strategy, the paper is divided in three parts

1. The note taking section: it contains all the relevant information recorded from the lesson.

2. The review section: it contains key points from the lesson. A student can jot down questions or points that might appear on the test.

3. The summary section: the student summarizes the information on the page to asssess what has been learned and to ask questions about materials that remain unclear. A sample Cornell Notes is provided next, but as students evolve in their studies, they progressively adopt more complicated note-taking strategies.

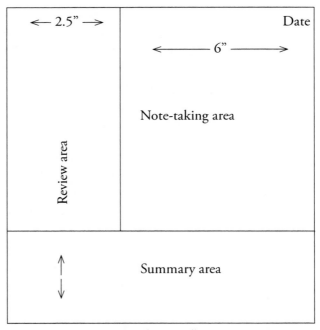

Figure 1: Sample Cornell notes page

o Typing or writing: improve the typing or writing speed enable the student to record as much information as possible during lectures. Notes should be organized efficiently for the student's benefit. Students with disabilities eligible for a scribe should self-disclose with the disability office in college to secure this accommodation if it would facilitate their learning.

• Study Skills

Our contemporary world is very noisy. Distractions abound and some students struggle to strike a balance when it comes to their studies. Though individuals are unique, some common rules might help students enjoy the greatest benefit from their review time.

- o Environment: determine the most comfortable environment to study. It can range from the school, the library, or a room at home. Regardless of preference, the environment should be as quiet as possible and void of distractions. Electronic devices (cellphones, tablets) should be set aside to maximize concentration.
- o Schedule: the student should have a regular study schedule based on personal activities and chores. It can vary from a school day to weekend but consistency such as after school or after dinner would be helpful.
- o Productivity: begin with the most difficult subjects when the brain is sharper and end with the easiest ones when the fatigue begins to set in. Take breaks if necessary and if tired, stop and appreciate the work accomplished.

- Test Taking Skills

So long as one gets a formal education, tests are a reality of life. Regardless of types of questions (essay, multiple choice, fill-in the blanks, matching, true or false, open book) students should read the instructions carefully to minimize the risk of errors. They must learn to scan the information quickly and familiarize themselves with all options prior to making a final decision. They should try as much as possible not to leave questions unanswered. For essay questions, a common tip recommends to create an outline with a clear thesis or argument, paragraphs and supporting evidence before starting the draft. Outlines help facilitate the brainstorm process and structure the final draft. Last but not the least, time management during the test is key for optimum performance. Therefore, students should study diligently or practice on a regular basis prior to every test they take. As a best practice, students should make some introspection meaning they should examine their test performance to determine area of improvement for future tests.

- Computer Skills

Nowadays, computer literacy is essential both at school and at work. The more programs and software students can operate efficiently, the more marketable they can become. More, research skills using the Internet and other available databases can propel a prospective job seeker at the top of candidates for interview.

- Communication Skills

Students should hone on both their oral and written communication skills. Though conversations might embrace informal language, students must be accustomed to formal language used in professional settings meaning they need to be able to convey their thoughts properly in writing. Furthermore, they need to practice their public speaking skills at every opportunity: class projects, school fairs, debate club, or student ambassador. Strong writing skills are equally necessary to produce quality essays for college applications and scholarships.

- Self-awareness Skills

High school students are growing teenagers learning about themselves and how they can thrive in their environment. Self-awareness involves knowing one's strengths and weaknesses, and being able to assess those of their interlocutors. One of the major advantages of self-awareness is its ability to stimulate self-control within individuals. A person knowledgeable of his or her triggers can avoid contentious situations with other people.

- Self-advocacy Skills

Unlike high school where educators provide students with all resources for success, in college, students must take the necessary steps to ensure that their needs are met. As early as 9th grade, they should practice seeking for help when needed. They should feel comfortable requesting a meeting with an administrator, a counselor, teacher, social worker, librarian or other school's staff without apprehension. Once in college, students would rely on that skill to seek support beginning with their advisor. Self-advocacy encourages students to be their own spokespersons. School administrators interact constantly with many students, and if students fail to voice their demands, their issues would not be addressed properly. If a student wants to discuss an issue that requires absolute confidentiality, he or she must inform the counselor prior to the beginning of the conversation. The last item on self-advocacy is to exhibit confidence. Some people are shy while others are talkative. Regardless of one's personality, every person should at least be able to share an opinion respectfully without being insolent.

- Résumé

It is difficult to predict when opportunity will knock. Students should maintain updated résumés listing their education, work, volunteer, and professional experience, additional skills, awards, or any other achievements. Résumés come in various formats. The following two samples provide information about two graduating seniors.

As a rule, students should keep their résumé limited to a single page. On the first sample (Dana Williams), the student highlights her GPA and courses that demonstrate exposure to a challenging curriculum i.e. AP Courses and Honors Courses. Some students underestimate their babysitting experience as unworthy to be included on their résumé. It should be included as it provides an insight into their trustworthiness. In the second résumé (Robin Jones), the student highlights the relevant coursework to her engineering program. Likewise, volunteer work and extracurricular activities are included in chronological order starting with the most recent. The computer skills listed further emphasize the engineering background of the student and can be connected to the coursework.

Dana Williams
1245 Main Street Apt # 10
City, State, Zip Code
Cellular Phone: 555-555-5555
Email: dana.williams@domain.com

EDUCATION
Success High School (Class of 2017)   City, State
Humanities Magnet Program
AP Coursework
- AP Language and Composition
- AP Biology
- AP Spanish Literature
- AP Psychology

Honors Coursework
- Honors Algebra
- Honors Chemistry

GPA
- Unweighted: 3.5
- Weighted: 4.03

WORK EXPERIENCE
Babysitter (Summer 2014)   Babies' Smiles Day Care   City, State
- Engage in fun activities with children ages 3 to 5
- Clean up the room at the end of the day

VOLUNTEER EXPERIENCE
Office Assistant (2015-2016)   Heart of the Community   City, State
- Reception coverage
- File applications of new clients to the program
- Prepare folders for volunteers' orientation

SKILLS
- Computer: Microsoft Word, Excel, PowerPoint,
- Programming: Java, Flash, HTML
- Languages: Spanish, Chinese

EXTRACURRICULAR ACTIVITIES
- Debate Club
- Newspaper Club
- Lacrosse Team
- Swimming Team

ACHIEVEMENTS & AWARDS
- County Young Leader Award (Junior Year)
- Athletic Scholar Award (Sophomore Year)
- Honor Roll Award (Freshman to Junior Years)

HOBBIES
- Reading, dancing

ROBIN JONES

2020 Whitfield Lane
City, State Zip Code
Cellular Phone: 555-555-5555
Email: Robinjones@domain.com

Education
- Success High School, City, State
- Engineering Magnet Program
- Expected Graduation Date: June 2017
- GPA 3.8 (unweighted), 4.12 (weighted)

Relevant Coursework
- Introduction to Engineering Design
- Principles of Engineering
- Digital Electronics
- Aerospace and Civil Engineering

Internship Experience
- STEM summer program at the State University (2016)
- Engineers of the Future Program (2015)

Volunteer Work
- Usher at Shakespeare Theater (2016-2017)
- City Public Library Volunteer once a week (2015-2016)
- Sandwich Preparer at St. Vincent Food Bank (Martin Luther King Day 2015)
- Active Youth Day (Summer 2014)
- Feeding the Homeless (Thanksgiving 2013)

Extracurricular Activities
- International Dance Team (2016-2017)
- Robotics Team (2015-2017)
- Debate Club (2014-2015)
- Varsity Soccer Team (2015)
- Green Team (2014)

Computer Skills
- Microsoft Office Suite (Word, Excel, PowerPoint, Publisher)
- Inventor (3D CAD Software)
- Robot C
- Autodesk Revit for architectural designs

Awards
- Honor Roll (9-12 grades)
- AP Scholar (2015)

- Job Search Skills

As a graduation requirement, students must complete community service or internships. The approaches they use to secure a position i.e. through their personal network (family, friends, teachers), community resources (job boards) or online remain the tools they would utilize in college and beyond. In college, the career center would become critical in their search for job opportunities. They should exercise caution if they decide to register with headhunter organizations because personal information might be required for their profiles.

- Interview Skills

Even for seasoned professionals, interviews are a daunting task. However, there are some tips high school students can easily follow to make the experience less intimidating. Prior to the interview, students should research the company, the position they are applying for, and assess their professional assets and areas for improvement. On the day of the interview, they must arrive early (usually 15 minutes prior to the meeting time), exhibit and maintain a professional demeanor the entire time they are around the business. They should remember that everyone, from the receptionist who greets them on arrival to the interviewer, is observing their behavior. They should shake the interviewer's hand firmly. During the interview, they should be prepared to share why the job is of interest to them and what contributions they would bring to the organization. Throughout the process, interviewees should watch their body language, the tone and pitch of their voice, and constantly maintain eye contact. At the end of the interview, students should ask some questions about the job such as training, performance evaluation and opportunities for growth. After the interview, it is customary and professional to send a thank you letter to the interviewer and reinforce the candidate's desire to work for their organization.

- Professionalism

Regardless of background, belief, and educational achievement, there is a certain code of conduct expected at the workplace. Proper attire, telephone and email etiquette, customer service, collaboration and teamwork, critical thinking, the ability to follow instructions and use feedback for growth are some key values of the job market with which students must become familiar. Similarly, individuals who take initiative in attempts to solve problems are highly valued.

By the time they leave high school, students must have mastered some of the basic of career readiness.

The school's curriculum might not allocate equal amounts of time for college readiness and career readiness. Nevertheless, both are equally important to shape a well-rounded student likely to graduate from college in a timely manner, in a major of interest, and to become a productive member of society. Success is a mindset that translates into action. Most of the time, successful students exhibit the following attributes:

- Driven/motivated
- Respectful
- Willing to learn
- Honest
- Optimistic
- Resourceful
- Flexible/adaptable
- Hard working
- Proactive
- Set high expectations

Student: _____   Grade: _____

Student Worksheet # 1 – Chapter 10

College Readiness Assessment

Purpose: Provide the student with an awareness of their personal competencies to succeed in college. Be as truthful as you can to evaluate your strengths and areas of improvement.

Academics

Rate the mastery of your skills in each of the high school listed courses below. Please select the last option if the statement doesn't apply to you.

• Algebra	○ Poor	○ Average	○ Good	○ Excellent	○ I don't know
• Architecture	○ Poor	○ Average	○ Good	○ Excellent	○ I don't know
• Art	○ Poor	○ Average	○ Good	○ Excellent	○ I don't know
• Art History	○ Poor	○ Average	○ Good	○ Excellent	○ I don't know
• Auto Body Repair Technology	○ Poor	○ Average	○ Good	○ Excellent	○ I don't know
• Auto Technology	○ Poor	○ Average	○ Good	○ Excellent	○ I don't know
• Biology	○ Poor	○ Average	○ Good	○ Excellent	○ I don't know
• Business/Finance	○ Poor	○ Average	○ Good	○ Excellent	○ I don't know
• Calculus	○ Poor	○ Average	○ Good	○ Excellent	○ I don't know
• Carpentry	○ Poor	○ Average	○ Good	○ Excellent	○ I don't know
• Chemistry	○ Poor	○ Average	○ Good	○ Excellent	○ I don't know
• Computer Science	○ Poor	○ Average	○ Good	○ Excellent	○ I don't know
• Construction Electricity	○ Poor	○ Average	○ Good	○ Excellent	○ I don't know
• Cosmetology	○ Poor	○ Average	○ Good	○ Excellent	○ I don't know
• Digital Graphics	○ Poor	○ Average	○ Good	○ Excellent	○ I don't know
• Early Childhood Development	○ Poor	○ Average	○ Good	○ Excellent	○ I don't know
• English	○ Poor	○ Average	○ Good	○ Excellent	○ I don't know
• Environmental Science	○ Poor	○ Average	○ Good	○ Excellent	○ I don't know
• Health	○ Poor	○ Average	○ Good	○ Excellent	○ I don't know
• Horticulture	○ Poor	○ Average	○ Good	○ Excellent	○ I don't know
• Hospitality & Tourism	○ Poor	○ Average	○ Good	○ Excellent	○ I don't know
• Human Geography	○ Poor	○ Average	○ Good	○ Excellent	○ I don't know
• HVAC [4]	○ Poor	○ Average	○ Good	○ Excellent	○ I don't know
• International Affairs/Relations	○ Poor	○ Average	○ Good	○ Excellent	○ I don't know
• Macroeconomics	○ Poor	○ Average	○ Good	○ Excellent	○ I don't know
• Marketing/Entrepreneurship	○ Poor	○ Average	○ Good	○ Excellent	○ I don't know
• Masonry	○ Poor	○ Average	○ Good	○ Excellent	○ I don't know

---

[4] Heating, Ventilation and Air Conditioning

• Microeconomics	○ Poor	○ Average	○ Good	○ Excellent	○ I don't know
• Music	○ Poor	○ Average	○ Good	○ Excellent	○ I don't know
• Network Technologies/Operations	○ Poor	○ Average	○ Good	○ Excellent	○ I don't know
• Performing Arts[5]	○ Poor	○ Average	○ Good	○ Excellent	○ I don't know
• Physics	○ Poor	○ Average	○ Good	○ Excellent	○ I don't know
• Physical Education	○ Poor	○ Average	○ Good	○ Excellent	○ I don't know
• Plumbing	○ Poor	○ Average	○ Good	○ Excellent	○ I don't know
• Politics	○ Poor	○ Average	○ Good	○ Excellent	○ I don't know
• Pre-Calculus	○ Poor	○ Average	○ Good	○ Excellent	○ I don't know
• Psychology	○ Poor	○ Average	○ Good	○ Excellent	○ I don't know
• Statistics	○ Poor	○ Average	○ Good	○ Excellent	○ I don't know
• US Government	○ Poor	○ Average	○ Good	○ Excellent	○ I don't know
• US History	○ Poor	○ Average	○ Good	○ Excellent	○ I don't know
• Visual Arts[6]	○ Poor	○ Average	○ Good	○ Excellent	○ I don't know
• World History	○ Poor	○ Average	○ Good	○ Excellent	○ I don't know
• World Languages[7]	○ Poor	○ Average	○ Good	○ Excellent	○ I don't know

---

[5]   Theater, dance, music, acting, musical production, video production
[6]   Ceramics, drawing, painting, photography, web design, 2D, 3D
[7]   Spanish, German, Japanese, Chinese, French, Italian, Russian, Arabic, Latin

By Stéphanie Mbella

Student Worksheet # 2 – Chapter 10

College General Curriculum Interest

Please select some general studies courses you would like to take in college.

Behavioral & Social Sciences

○ Anthropology	○ Geography	○ Political Science
○ Child Development	○ History	○ Psychology
○ Communication	○ Linguistics	○ Sociology
○ Economics	○ Marketing	

Humanities

○ Architecture	○ English	○ History
○ Archeology	○ Film Studies	○ Philosophy
○ Art	○ Foreign Languages	○ Religion

Mathematics

○ Advanced Mathematics	○ Finite Mathematics	○ Trigonometry
○ Calculus	○ Probability	
○ College Algebra	○ Statistics	

Performing Arts

○ Dance	○ Music	○ Theater

Science

○ Astronomy	○ Computer Science	○ Meteorology
○ Biology	○ Environment	○ Physics
○ Biochemistry	○ Geography	
○ Chemistry	○ Geology	

Visual Arts

○ Ceramics	○ Pottery	
○ Drawing	○ Sculpture	
○ Painting		
○ Photography		

Student Worksheet # 3 – Chapter 10

Skills for Success Assessment
Rate your skills for academic success in college

• Budgeting	○ Poor	○ Average	○ Good	○ Excellent	○ I don't know
• Communication	○ Poor	○ Average	○ Good	○ Excellent	○ I don't know
• Computer	○ Poor	○ Average	○ Good	○ Excellent	○ I don't know
• Goal setting	○ Poor	○ Average	○ Good	○ Excellent	○ I don't know
• Interview	○ Poor	○ Average	○ Good	○ Excellent	○ I don't know
• Investigative (lab)	○ Poor	○ Average	○ Good	○ Excellent	○ I don't know
• Job search	○ Poor	○ Average	○ Good	○ Excellent	○ I don't know
• Leadership	○ Poor	○ Average	○ Good	○ Excellent	○ I don't know
• Note taking	○ Poor	○ Average	○ Good	○ Excellent	○ I don't know
• Organization	○ Poor	○ Average	○ Good	○ Excellent	○ I don't know
• Presentation	○ Poor	○ Average	○ Good	○ Excellent	○ I don't know
• Problem Solving	○ Poor	○ Average	○ Good	○ Excellent	○ I don't know
• Professionalism	○ Poor	○ Average	○ Good	○ Excellent	○ I don't know
• Public Speaking	○ Poor	○ Average	○ Good	○ Excellent	○ I don't know
• Reading	○ Poor	○ Average	○ Good	○ Excellent	○ I don't know
• Research	○ Poor	○ Average	○ Good	○ Excellent	○ I don't know
• Résumé	○ Poor	○ Average	○ Good	○ Excellent	○ I don't know
• Self-advocacy	○ Poor	○ Average	○ Good	○ Excellent	○ I don't know
• Self-awareness	○ Poor	○ Average	○ Good	○ Excellent	○ I don't know
• Study	○ Poor	○ Average	○ Good	○ Excellent	○ I don't know
• Test taking	○ Poor	○ Average	○ Good	○ Excellent	○ I don't know
• Time management	○ Poor	○ Average	○ Good	○ Excellent	○ I don't know
• Teamwork	○ Poor	○ Average	○ Good	○ Excellent	○ I don't know
• Writing	○ Poor	○ Average	○ Good	○ Excellent	○ I don't know

Student Worksheet # 4 – Chapter 10

Self-Reflection – College Readiness Level

Key Points	Responses
When you reflect on your previous answers, how confident are you with your college preparedness level?	☐ Very confident ☐ Confident ☐ Partly confident ☐ Not confident
What's your plan to be even more prepared before you start college in the fall after your high school graduation?	_____ _____ _____ _____ _____
Based on your skills for success assessment in the previous exercise, list the subjects in which you perform best.	1. _____ 2. _____ 3. _____ 4. _____
Based on your skills for success assessment in the previous exercise, list the subjects in which you struggle the most.	1. _____ 2. _____ 3. _____ 4. _____
Based on your skills for success assessment in the previous exercise, list your strongest skills.	1. _____ 2. _____ 3. _____ 4. _____
Based on your skills for success assessment in the previous exercise, list your weakest skills.	1. _____ 2. _____ 3. _____ 4. _____
How do you plan to improve your weakest skills?	_____ _____ _____ _____ _____

Parent Worksheet # 5 – Chapter 10

Parent self-reflection

Key Points	Responses
How confident are you with your child's college preparedness level?	☐ Very confident ☐ Confident ☐ Partly confident ☐ Not confident
How confident are you with your child's career preparedness level?	☐ Very confident ☐ Confident ☐ Partly confident ☐ Not confident
Rate your child's strongest college readiness skills Reading Writing Mathematics Science Social Studies Test taking Notetaking	1. _____ 2. _____ 3. _____ 4. _____ 5. _____ 6. _____ 7. _____
Rate your child's strongest career readiness skills Resume writing Cover letter Customer service Job search Reference request	1. _____ 2. _____ 3. _____ 4. _____ 5. _____
Rate your child's business competencies skills from the strongest to the weakest Goal setting Organization Time management Computer Communication Planning Problem solving Public speaking Teamwork Professionalism Critical thinking Self-awareness Self-advocacy	1. _____ 2. _____ 3. _____ 4. _____ 5. _____ 6. _____ 7. _____ 8. _____ 9. _____ 10. _____ 11. _____ 12. _____ 13. _____

Conclusion

The goal of this guide is to provide a quick snapshot of the American High School landscape using examples from the Greater Washington District Metro Area. The intrinsic structure of the high school system herein presented remains somehow similar in many localities across the United States. In addition to this general overview, parents and students should seek updated information from their local high school. Information constantly changes based on new realities. Nevertheless, they should grasp the fact that academic performance, extra-curricular activities, standardized test scores along with a quality application constitutes the foundation for a strong college application package. Regardless of multiple obligations, parental involvement is critical to a student's academic success. Parents should carve out time in their schedule to provide the emotional and financial support their offspring would need. The college application process begins in 9th grade and continues throughout high school. If not planned well, it can become costly, complicated, and arduous. However, with good preparation, many of the frustrations can be mitigated so that the student ends up at the school that is the best academic, social, and financial fit. College readiness and career readiness remain the most common benchmarks used to assess the level of preparation of teenagers transitioning into the post-high school world. Upon graduation, all students should have mastered skills conducive to success and growth in both the academic and professional worlds. Although students might not learn all skills in a classroom setting, they can be acquired through exposure to professional environments such as internships, community service, and jobs. Regardless of the student's academic performance, emotional readiness and financial readiness constitute potent factors likely to impact college readiness and career readiness, and ultimately the student's final college selection.

At the end of this piece, my hope is that immigrant parents and their offspring would feel more empowered to navigate the local high school system and parents to become more involved in the academic endeavor of their offspring. They should feel comfortable to seek help when needed. By utilizing all resources available, they can avoid making life-changing decisions based on erroneous information or assumptions.

Resources for College Planning

The following resources are given as a reference. Parents and students should check each website for its veracity, updates, and to ensure that its content meets their needs.

College search
- Big Future by College Board:
  https://bigfuture.collegeboard.org/college-search
- Chegg: https://www.chegg.com/schools
- College Confidential: http://www.collegeconfidential.com/college_search/
- College Data:
  http://www.collegedata.com/cs/search/college/college_search_tmpl.jhtml
- College Navigator: https://nces.ed.gov/collegenavigator/
- College View: http://www.collegeview.com/collegesearch/index.jsp
- CollegeWeek Live: http://www.collegeweeklive.com/
- CSO College Center: http://www.imfirst.org/
- Hispanic Association of Colleges and Universities (HACU):
  www.hacu.net
- Historically Black Colleges and Universities (HBCU):
  http://hbcuconnect.com/colleges/
- Niche : https://colleges.niche.com/?degree=4-year&sort=best
- Southern Regional Education Board (Academic Common Market): http://www.sreb.org/academic-common-market
- U101 College Search: http://u101.com/

Information for student athletes
- The National Collegiate Athletic Association (NCAA): http://www.ncaa.org/

College search and scholarship opportunities
- College Board: https://bigfuture.collegeboard.org/scholarship-search
- College Greenlight: https://www.collegegreenlight.com/
- Cappex: https://www.cappex.com/
- Fastweb: http://colleges.fastweb.com/
- Peterson's: https://www.petersons.com/
- Unigo: https://www.unigo.com/

College Applications
- Common Application: http://www.commonapp.org/
- Coalition for Access, Affordability, and Success: http://www.coalitionforcollegeaccess.org/

Citations in Essays
- http://www.easybib.com/
- http://www.bibme.org/

Standardized Testing
- ACT: https://www.act.org/
- SAT: https://collegereadiness.collegeboard.org/sat
- TOEFL: https://www.ets.org/toefl/
- AP Exams: https://apstudent.collegeboard.org/home
- Accuplacer Test: https://accuplacer.collegeboard.org/student/practice

Scholarship Search Engines
- www.scholarshipsonline.org
- www.scholarships.com
- https://www.raise.me/

Dreamers Scholarships
- The Dream.US Scholarship: http://www.thedream.us/
- The Esperanza Education Fund Scholarship: http://www.esperanzafund.org/

Scholarships for Students of Immigrant Families
- The Esperanza Education Fund Scholarship: http://www.esperanzafund.org/

National Annual scholarships
- Horatio Alger Scholarship Programs
  https://scholars.horatioalger.org/scholarships/about-our-scholarship-programs/
- Jack Kent Cooke Scholarship Programs: http://www.jkcf.org/scholarship-programs/
- Jackie Robinson : https://www.jackierobinson.org/apply/
- Ron Brown: https://www.ronbrown.org/
- QuestBridge: https://www.questbridge.org/
- Posse (nominations required): https://www.possefoundation.org/

DMV Annual Scholarships
- Thursday Network "I Empower Scholarship" https://thursdaynetwork.org/
- Junior Achievement Essay: http://www.myja.org/essay/
- New Future Scholarships: https://www.newfuturesdc.org/
- HBCU Council of Shiloh Baptist Church in Washington DC: http://www.hbcucouncil.com/Scholarship.html

Minorities Scholarships
- African American
  o NAACP Scholarships: http://www.naacp.org/naacp-scholarships/
  o United Negro Fund Scholarships: https://www.uncf.org/
- Hispanic/Latino
  o Hispanic Scholarship Fund: https://www.hsf.net/
  o Maldef Scholarships: http://www.maldef.org/leadership/scholarships/index.html

By STÉPHANIE MBELLA

Professional organizations scholarships

- National Action Council for Minorities in Engineering:
  http://www.nacme.org/
- National Society of Black Engineers:
  https://connect.nsbe.org/Scholarships/ScholarshipList.aspx

Virtual Campus Tours

- Campus Tours: http://www.campustours.com/
- CollegeWeek Live: http://www.collegeweeklive.com/

State Education Agencies

- District of Columbia State Board of Education:
  http://sboe.dc.gov/
- Maryland State Department of Education:
  http://www.marylandpublicschools.org/Pages/default.aspx
- Virginia Department of Education: http://www.doe.virginia.gov/

Financial Aid

- To create an FSA ID: https://fsaid.ed.gov/npas/index.htm
- FAFSA : https://fafsa.ed.gov/
- US Department of Education: http://www.ed.gov/
- CSS Profile: https://student.collegeboard.org/css-financial-aid-profile
- Financial Aid Glossary: https://studentaid.ed.gov/sa/glossary
- FAFSA4CASTER: https://fafsa.ed.gov/FAFSA/app/
  f4cForm?execution=e2s1

State Aid

- DCTAG (DC Tuition Assistance Grant): http://osse.dc.gov/dctag
- MD-CAPS (Maryland Higher Education Commission):
  http://mhec.maryland.gov/Pages/default.aspx
- VA TAG (Virginia Tuition Assistance Grant):
  http://www.cicv.org/Affordability/Tuition-Assistance-Grant.aspx

Career Information

- The Princeton Review: http://www.princetonreview.com/career-search

- US Bureau of Labor Statistics for job outlook:
  http://www.bls.gov/ooh/

Career Assessments

- Your Free Career Test: http://www.yourfreecareertest.com/
- The Princeton Review: http://www.princetonreview.com/quiz/career-quiz

References

ACT

American University

Bowie State University

California State University Los Angeles

Coalition for Access, Affordability, and Success

College Board

College of Williams and Mary

Community College of the District of Columbia

Common Application

Council for American Private Education (CAPE)

DC Charter School Board

District of Columbia Public Schools

Fairfax County Public Schools

Federal Student Aid

Friend, Marilyn Penovich. *Co-Teach!: Building and Sustaining Effective Classroom Partnerships in Inclusive Schools.* Greensboro, NC: 2013.

Frostburg State University

Gallaudet University

George Washington University

George Mason University

Georgetown University

Goucher College

Hampton University

Hawaii Public Schools

Hollins University

Howard University

Internal Revenue Service Qualified Tuition Program (QTP)

Johns Hopkins University

By Stéphanie Mbella

Liberty University
Longwood University
Loyola University of Maryland
Khan Academy
Magnet Schools of America
Maryland Department of Education
Maryland Higher Education Commission
McDaniel College
Myers, Isabel Briggs, and Peter B. Myers. *Gifts Differing: Understanding Personality Type*. Mountain View, CA: CPP, 1995.
Myers-Briggs Personality Test
Montgomery College
Montgomery County Public Schools
Morgan State University
Mount St. Mary's University
National Charter School Resource Center
National Association for College Admission Counseling (NACAC)
National Dissemination Center for Children with Disabilities (NICHCY)
National Education Association (NEA)
Northern Virginia Community College
Old Dominion University
Office of the State Superintendent of Education – Washington DC
Ohio Higher Ed – Department of Higher Education: Adult Basic and Literacy Education (ABLE)
OuYang, Benjamin T. Director, Department of Career Readiness and Innovative Programs, Montgomery County Public Schools
Prince George's Community College
Prince George's County Public Schools
Randolph-Macon College
Salisbury University
Shenandoah University
State Council of Higher Education for Virginia
The Catholic University of America
The National Center for Fair & Open Testing
Towson University

188

Trinity University of Washington DC
United States Department of Education
University of Maryland Baltimore County
University of Maryland College Park
University of the District of Columbia
University of Oklahoma Career Services
US Bureau of Labor Statistics
University of Richmond
University of Virginia
Virginia Commonwealth University
Virginia Department of Education
Virginia Tech
World-Class Instructional Design and Assessment (WIDA)

Websites

British School of Washington DC: http://www.nordangliaeducation.com/our-schools/washington

Deutsche Schule – German School Washington DC: http://www.dswashington.org/

FairTest: The National Center for Fair & Open Testing: http://www.fairtest.org/

International education-International Baccalaureate: http://www.ibo.org/

Khan Academy: https://www.khanacademy.org/

Lycée Rochambeau French International School: http://www.rochambeau.org/

Partnership for Assessment of Readiness for College and Careers: http://www.parcconline.org/

www.edutopia.org

www.iseek.org (A Minnesota State Colleges and Universities Career and Education Resource)

https://collegereadiness.collegeboard.org/sat/inside-the-test/compare-new-sat-act

http://www.familyeducation.com/school/admission-interviews/

top-10-things-colleges-look-high-school-student

Appendices

Appendix 1: Sample College Applications Tracker

School & State	Admission Types	Categories	Application Types	Date Transcript Requests Submitted	Date Recommendation Letters Submitted	Date ACT Scores sent to Colleges	Date SAT Scores sent to Colleges	Date Application submitted to College	Date Application Fee Waiver or Payment sent to Colleges

Admission Types

ED = Early Decision   EA = Earlier Action   ERA = Early Restricted Action   RD = Regular Decision   ROA = Rolling Admission

School Categories   R = Reach School   T = Target School   S = Safety School

Application Types   SA = School Application   CA = Common Application   CAAS = Coalition Application

Optional requirements

- Date Mid-Year Report sent to Colleges: _____
- Date TOEFL Scores sent to Colleges: _____

Appendix 2: Sample Financial Aid Application Tracker

Colleges/ Universities	CSS Profile Submission Dates (if applicable)	FAFSA Submission Date	SAR (Student Aid Report) Reception Date	State Grants Applications Submission Dates (if applicable)	Senators Scholarship Applications Submission Dates (if applicable)	Delegates Scholarship Applications Submission Dates (if applicable)

Appendix 3: Sample Scholarship Applications Tracker

Name of Scholarship	Types Merit-based (M) Need-based (N) Athletic-based (A) Community Service (CS) Other (O)	Organization/ Sponsor/ Administrator	Contacts for questions	Award Amount	Submission Deadlines	Application Submission Dates

Endnotes

1   SSAT: Secondary School Administration Test
2   ISEE: Independence School Entrance Exam
3   OLSAT: Otis-Lennon Ability Test
4   SCAT: School and College Ability Test
5   HSPT: High School Placement Test
6   Unlike Francophone countries which educational system has experienced few revisions from the colonial era, many English-speaking countries have revamped their school system. Some have 7 to 8 years in elementary schools and 6 years in secondary schools. This table is provided for illustrative purposes only.
7   Test costs for the 2016-2017 Academic Year
8   UDC does not offer on campus housing to students.

CPSIA information can be obtained
at www.ICGtesting.com
Printed in the USA
LVOW07s1140210817
545791LV00001B/119/P